LEADERS *Helping* LEADERS

CORWIN
PRESS

JOHN C. DARESH

LEADERS
Helping
LEADERS

SECOND EDITION

A PRACTICAL GUIDE TO
ADMINISTRATIVE MENTORING

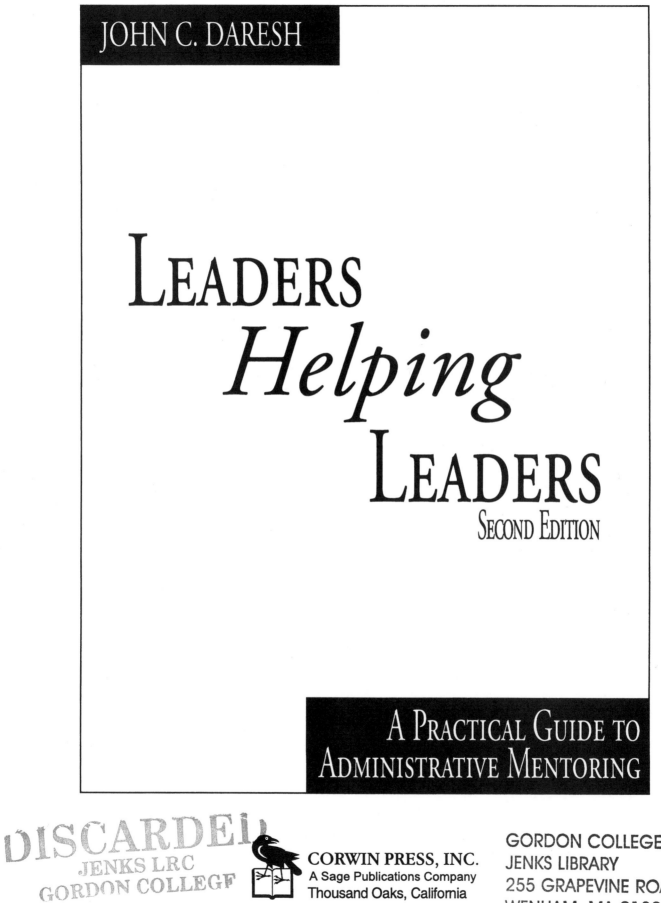

CORWIN PRESS, INC.
A Sage Publications Company
Thousand Oaks, California

For information:

Corwin Press, Inc.,
A Sage Publications Company
2455 Teller Road
Thousand Oaks, California 91320
e-mail: order@corwinpress.com

SAGE Publications Ltd.
6 Bonhill Street
London EC2A 4PU
United Kingdom

Sage Publications India Pvt. Ltd.
M-32 Market
Greater Kailash I
New Delhi 110 048 India

Printed in the United States of America

Library of Congress Cataloging-in-Publication Data

Daresh, John C.
    Leaders helping leaders: A practical guide to administrative
mentoring / by John C. Daresh.—2nd ed.
        p.   cm.
    Includes bibliographical references and index.
    ISBN 0-7619-7779-1 (c : alk. paper)—ISBN 0-7619-7780-5
(p : alk. paper)
    1. Mentoring in education United States. 2. School
administrators — In-service training United States. I. Title.
LB1731.4 .D37 2000
371.2'011'—dc21 00   010500

This book is printed on acid-free paper.

    04 05 06 07 7 6 5 4

Editorial Assistant: Kylee Liegl
Acquiring Editor: Robb Clouse
Production Editor: Diane S. Foster
Editorial Assistant: Candice Crocetti
Typesetter/Designer: D&G Limited, LLC
Cover Designer: Michelle Lee

Contents

About the Author

John C. Daresh is Professor of Educational Leadership at the University of Texas at El Paso. He has worked in faculty and administrative positions in higher education for the past 20 years at the University of Cincinnati, The Ohio State University, the University of Northern Colorado, and now in Texas. He has worked as a consultant for school districts, universities, and state departments of education across the United States, Europe, Africa, and Asia. Over the years, he has authored more than 100 articles, books, book chapters, and papers dealing with the professional development of school leaders. He began his career by working in private and public schools in Dubuque, Iowa and Chicago. He received his doctorate from the University of Wisconsin at Madison.

Introduction

As CONTROVERSIES RAGE over which educational practices are most likely to improve schools, one constant factor is often overlooked. Leadership makes effective organizations, and this statement is also true of what contributes most directly to quality in schools. Arguments that are related to more effective approaches to reading and math take place across the country and around the world. There is a reality that does not change, however, regardless of whether a school is located in Massachusetts, Indiana, New Mexico, Johannesburg, or Taipei. Schools work better when they have strong leaders. Although few would argue the centrality of effective leadership as a key ingredient in good schools, other realities exist that make it more difficult to ensure the continuation of this critical component. First, schools are losing their leaders at an alarming rate across the United States and throughout the world. Early retirements are luring many out of the principal's office, and school systems are continuing to grow. It is difficult to keep up with the increasing demand for more leaders. Second, the job of being a school leader is becoming more complex each day. The traditional role of the principal as the person who must simply shuffle a few papers, evaluate teachers now and then, and maintain discipline is long gone. Also, superintendents are thrown into constant battles over budgets, politics, and labor problems. Finally, fewer people want the hassle of being a school administrator. Teacher salaries rise at a rate that makes it less appealing to become principals and superintendents—and to take on their problems.

This book is intended to help you develop a comprehensive approach to providing more effective professional development opportunities for the leaders in your school and district. At the outset, it must be acknowledged that mentoring for school administrators is but one approach to providing assistance that might alleviate some of the problems resulting from the issues noted previously. Simply having a mentoring program for beginning and experienced principals and central office administrators will not reduce the need for more leaders over the next few years, nor will it make the job of a school leader any easier. It will not even guarantee that people will now begin to leap at the opportunity to become assistant principals or superintendents. But mentoring for school leaders is meant to be at least one weapon in an arsenal of activities that could assist people who take on the challenges of trying to make a difference in schools. If school systems can find ways of bringing talented people together in order to learn from each other, there will be a noticeable effect on leadership in their schools. The job of the administrator might not be quite as lonely. There might be ways in which people who are working together can tackle some of the dilemmas that face our leaders. And, in general, the job of being a leader in schools might become a bit more appealing to talented people who want to make improvements in the quality of educational practice.

This book is designed to assist school district and even individual school personnel with considering a number of issues that are related to the development of an effective mentoring program for school administrators. A three-phase model is presented in order to lead you through initial planning, implementation, and evaluation issues. The chapters are filled with suggested issues and activities to assist you with developing effective programs at the local level.

Mentoring is an important part of effective administrator professional development. But you are alerted here to the fact that it cannot be viewed as the panacea that will solve all problems facing leaders. School systems need to work collaboratively with state departments of education, local universities, and many other different educational and non-educational agencies in order to explore better ways of attracting talented people to administration and leadership. More effective recruitment and pre-service programs must be designed. Also, sufficient resources need to be directed toward helping the leaders of learning activities in schools continue their own development and growth.

PART I

PLANNING THE MENTORING PROGRAM FOR SCHOOL LEADERS

LESLIE CHIN reflected on this past school year—the first in which she served as the superintendent of schools. Although it had generally been a very positive and rewarding experience (a fact that was recently confirmed by her evaluation conference with the school board), she reflected on a number of concerns as she contemplated the next year.

One issue that troubled her was the problem of feeling so alone. Leslie had served as a high school principal in the past, so she already knew that school administrators are often isolated from colleagues. But she did have some peers who were close to her in the district. Other principals were just a phone call away, and they shared many of the same problems and concerns that she did. She now realized that as the superintendent, she was the chief executive officer of the district and she had no immediate peers. Furthermore, the superintendents in neighboring districts also felt isolated in their jobs, but no one ever tried to step over district boundaries to talk or work with other superintendents.

Where could she turn to find someone who was open and honest enough to tell her how she was doing as a superintendent? How could she get in touch with people who would help her, answer the thousands of questions that she had, and who would have a friendly lunch with her but not engage in the kind of verbal one-upmanship that is so characteristic of the conversation at many formal meetings of area superintendents? Was it possible that all of the others were completely satisfied with the work that they were doing?

A few blocks away from Leslie's office, we find Roosevelt Adams, an elementary school principal in the district for nine years. From the outside, it would be almost impossible to tell that Roosevelt was not thoroughly happy and satisfied with his work. He often makes public statements such as, "The principalship is always what I wanted to reach, and it's the job I plan to leave when I retire from education." Most observers do not realize how often Roosevelt sits in his office trying to figure out what new challenges will come to him so that he can move beyond the stagnation he has felt during the past two years. What about a central office job? Should he transfer to a bigger school? What about finding a job in another district? At the age of 45, retirement is not really an option, but on occasion, Roosevelt even thinks about walking away from professional education and finding a job in private industry.

Mentoring: A Possible Answer

Both of these scenarios are fairly typical of the place where many school administrators find themselves at one time or another during their careers. Educators know that the world of the superintendent or principal, although exciting, challenging, and often personally rewarding, is also a world filled with considerable anxiety, frustration, self-doubt, and loneliness. But there is also a corresponding part of the world of school administrators in many school systems that proclaims, "You're the boss. Fix your own problems, and don't ask for help from anyone. If you can't do the job on your own, you're a failure." Indeed, the image of the leader as the Lone Ranger is very much alive in the world of school administration.

This book proposes an alternative to the concept of sink-or-swim survival in school administration. It might not be in anyone's best interest to assume that only the strongest and most self-reliant should survive as school leaders.

Instead, asking for help when it is needed is an example of strength, not weakness. There is nothing wrong with having a system where the norm is for leaders to help other leaders. These assumptions are made because of another core belief: School administrators are important people who do important jobs, and as a result, all of the different forms of help that can be made available to these key actors should be promoted.

The form of support promoted in the chapters that follow is professional development through the use of mentoring. Individual school districts, intermediate educational agencies, state departments of education, or universities can serve leaders in the field by planning, implementing, and evaluating formal mentoring programs that will enable school administrators to find helpful colleagues on an ongoing basis.

Part I of the book presents information that will be useful to you as you plan for the implementation of a structured mentoring program in order to support educational leaders in your district. Information is included about the definitions and purposes of mentoring, the benefits that are normally derived from mentoring, and the kinds of training programs that are available to assist school system planners with the design of local mentor preparation programs. At the end of Part I, you will be invited to sketch out the details of a plan for establishing a mentoring program for the leaders in your district.

1

What Is Mentoring, and Why Is It So Important?

THIS OPENING CHAPTER will help you understand what mentoring is and what it can do for your school system and for the people who work as your educational leaders.

Mentoring is an ongoing process in which individuals in an organization provide support and guidance to others who can become effective contributors to the goals of the organization. Unlike many other views of mentoring, a mentor does not necessarily have to be an older person who is ready, willing, and able to provide all of the answers to those who are newcomers. Usually, mentors have a lot of experience and craft knowledge to share with others. But the notion that good mentoring consists of a sage who directs the work of the less experienced to the point that no one will make any mistakes is not reasonable. As we will explain in Chapter 4, "Who Is a Mentor?", being a mentor implies the responsibility of not only sharing but also of listening and learning. If your school adopts a mentoring program, the program must have the potential of helping those who are mentored (or protégés, a word that we will use throughout this book), those who serve as mentors, and also the school system that chooses to start a mentoring program.

Before reading the rest of this chapter, you should complete the Mentoring Background Quiz that follows. This quiz is designed to disclose your understanding of this topic.

The remaining chapters of this book will (a) help you gain a more complete view of what mentoring is, (b) explore some of the major issues associated with planning, implementing, and evaluating a mentoring program in your district, and (c) provide you with practical advice that is designed to make your program an important part of the leadership development efforts in your district.

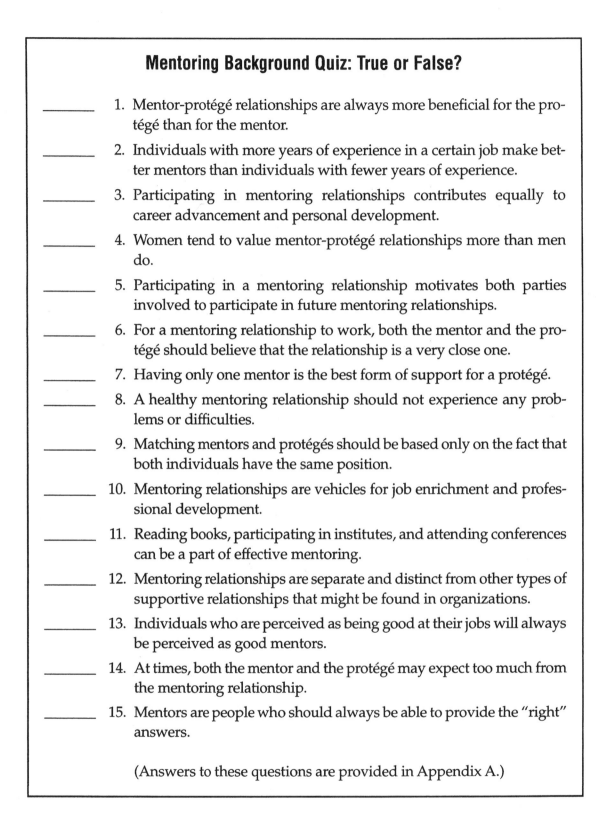

Mentoring Background Quiz: True or False?

_____   1. Mentor-protégé relationships are always more beneficial for the protégé than for the mentor.

_____   2. Individuals with more years of experience in a certain job make better mentors than individuals with fewer years of experience.

_____   3. Participating in mentoring relationships contributes equally to career advancement and personal development.

_____   4. Women tend to value mentor-protégé relationships more than men do.

_____   5. Participating in a mentoring relationship motivates both parties involved to participate in future mentoring relationships.

_____   6. For a mentoring relationship to work, both the mentor and the protégé should believe that the relationship is a very close one.

_____   7. Having only one mentor is the best form of support for a protégé.

_____   8. A healthy mentoring relationship should not experience any problems or difficulties.

_____   9. Matching mentors and protégés should be based only on the fact that both individuals have the same position.

_____   10. Mentoring relationships are vehicles for job enrichment and professional development.

_____   11. Reading books, participating in institutes, and attending conferences can be a part of effective mentoring.

_____   12. Mentoring relationships are separate and distinct from other types of supportive relationships that might be found in organizations.

_____   13. Individuals who are perceived as being good at their jobs will always be perceived as good mentors.

_____   14. At times, both the mentor and the protégé may expect too much from the mentoring relationship.

_____   15. Mentors are people who should always be able to provide the "right" answers.

(Answers to these questions are provided in Appendix A.)

Why Start a Mentoring Program?

If your district adopts a mentoring program, a strong commitment will be needed to support the effort. This effort does not necessarily imply a lot of money, however. In fact, over time, a district that has a mentoring program can actually save money. On the other hand, time must be devoted to mentor training, development, and opportunities in order for mentoring to take place. Adopting a program also means that a district accepts the fact that its administrators are more than building managers. They must be viewed as true professionals who have wisdom and experience to share with others.

If mentoring implies changes in attitudes and job descriptions, time commitment, and some financial support, why would you even consider this kind of a program? After all, most people recognize that change in education is extremely difficult to achieve, that time is the least available resource for administrators, and that few districts have a lot of extra money. Despite these obstacles, quality school systems promote mentoring programs because of the many benefits for school leaders, and these benefits are likely to be achieved by mentors, protégés, and school districts.

Benefits to Mentors

You probably experienced at some point in your life an informal process in your relationship with someone that might be described as mentoring. Your mentor might have been a favorite teacher in school, an athletic coach, an employer, or any other people who have made a difference in your personal or professional life. And you might have had a similar impact on the life of another person. You also might have served as a mentor.

Before you read about the common benefits, take a moment to reflect on some of the values that you have derived from serving as a mentor to others:

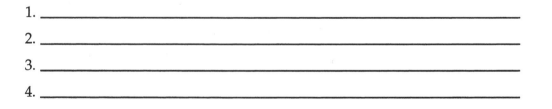

1. _____
2. _____
3. _____
4. _____

Now, compare your list with some of the benefits identified in the literature on this topic:

1. After serving in this role, mentors report greater overall satisfaction with their jobs as administrators. (Like any good teacher, a mentor learns as much as those who are mentored.)

2. Mentors get increased recognition from their peers. (People who get a reputation as being organizational helpers usually achieve a higher status in the system.)

3. Mentoring gives people opportunities for personal career advancement.

4. Mentors often gain a renewed enthusiasm for the profession. (Mentors often find that the things that they frequently take for granted become behaviors that are highly valued by others.)

In short, individuals who have served in a mentoring capacity to either aspiring or practicing administrative colleagues report that they have gained much in this type of relationship. Perhaps the best way to summarize this feeling is that despite the amount of time that is involved with maintaining an effective mentoring relationship, mentors express a desire to serve in this capacity again in the future.

Benefits to Protégés

You have likely been at the receiving end of a mentoring relationship at some point in your life, as well. What are some of the benefits that you have enjoyed as a result of someone serving as your mentor?

1. _____

2. _____

3. _____

4. _____

Individuals who have been protégés in formal mentoring programs for school administrators have identified the following benefits:

1. Protégés feel more confident about their professional competence (they find that others respect their work).

2. Protégés see theory translated into practice (they learn that it is possible for good ideas to be transformed into effective actions on the job).

3. Communication skills are enhanced. (Mentoring relationships lead to the creation of a climate of collegial support across the whole district.)

4. Mentoring is a way to learn the tricks of the trade.

5. Mentoring makes people feel as if they belong (it makes people feel as if others care about their personal and professional well-being).

In general, mentoring relationships—whether they naturally evolve through informal contact with someone (such as mentoring from a favorite teacher) or develop through a structured and formal program (such as mentoring for new principals in a school district)—are powerful learning opportunities. Protégés learn more about their professional lives and gain more insight into their personal needs, visions, and values than through any other kind of learning experience.

Benefits to Districts

School systems also gain from the implementation of mentoring programs for administrators.

What are some of the benefits that you see as possible for school districts that adopt mentoring?

1. _____

2. _____

3. _____

4. _____

School systems across the country have explored mentoring schemes and have identified the following benefits:

1. They have more capable staff. (Leaders in school systems that have mentoring programs tend to be energized by this practice.)

2. An attitude of lifelong learning is created among all administrators.

3. Higher motivation levels and job satisfaction are found in the staff. (More effective and enthusiastic managerial performance results when people understand that the system shows that they are worthy by establishing a mentoring program.)

4. The staff demonstrates an improved sense of self-esteem.

5. Greater productivity results. (As all of these other benefits are realized, people do their jobs better, and the organization is more productive.)

Potential Problems With Mentoring

Despite the great number of benefits that are likely to be achieved by mentors, protégés, and school districts, potential problems also need to be understood. Some of these problems are listed as follows. We also suggest ways in which the problems might be minimized. These problems are listed to make you aware of them, not to discourage you from adopting a mentoring program.

Possible Problem 1: Relationships that are too protective and controlling might be formed.

Potential Solution: At the outset, both the mentor and the protégés need to specify the precise level of support that is needed during the term of the mentoring relationship.

Possible Problem 2: Mentors who become advocates for protégés might ignore limitations.

Potential Solution: Mentors must constantly keep in mind that they are to support and help people in a realistic way—not create perfect, heroic images of their protégés.

Possible Problem 3: Mentors might become too demanding of the individuals with whom they work.

Potential Solution: A learning contract or other form of written agreement can be prepared at the outset of a mentoring relationship as a way to encourage the specification of expectations on the part of the mentor and protégés.

Possible Problem 4: Good leaders do not always make good mentors.

Potential Solution: School districts that establish mentoring programs must be careful to avoid the tendency to promote mentoring as a form of recognition or reward for administrators. Mentoring is hard work and implies a commitment to a special type of teaching that goes beyond simply reacting to others' questions.

Possible Problem 5: Protégés might develop a limited perspective on problem solving by relying too much on a single mentor.

Potential Solution: Protégés should be encouraged to find multiple mentors.

Possible Problem 6: Protégés might develop too great of a reliance on particular mentors.

Potential Solution: Districts can establish teams of mentors and encourage protégés to select different individuals for different skills that are found in the total team.

Possible Problem 7: Expectations that are established for mentoring relationships might be unrealistically high.

Potential Solution: Open communication at the outset between mentor and protégés, along with the development of a formal plan to guide the relationship, is essential to avoid misunderstandings in the future.

Possible Problem 8: Mentors and protégés often form very close relationships that will end eventually. Both parties feel a good deal of pain.

Possible Solution: Mentors and protégés need to talk to one another openly about the formation of long-term friendships that grow from the mentor-protégé relationship. Mentors and protégés become equals quickly, and with that development, partnerships that are based on parity might last for entire careers.

Summarizing the Chapter

This opening chapter provided a brief overview of and an orientation to the concept of mentoring as it can be used in your school system to support school leaders. Mentoring has the following characteristics:

- Is a powerful device to help leaders develop new insights into the profession

- Reduces isolation and helps build a collegial network among professional colleagues

- Helps move the novice from a level of mere survival to initial success when used with beginning administrators

2

Initial Program Development

ONCE YOU HAVE DECIDED to start a mentoring program in your school district, you need to address a number of key issues. Whenever any new program (such as a mentoring program for school administrators) is to be incorporated into a school system, certain preliminary activities must take place in order for the program to be accepted by school personnel—thus increasing its likelihood of being successful. This chapter includes information that you can use as you begin to plan a mentoring program. In addition, it presents an outline to assist planners of local mentoring programs with their design, implementation, and evaluation efforts.

Planning a Program: A Typical Case

Glenn Burbank was given the responsibility to develop an administrative mentoring program for the Shadyville School District. The district had never had much of a focus on professional development for school leaders in the past, so assigning someone to this task was a real change. Carlos Ramirez, the new superintendent, had indicated that leadership development would be given a high priority. The problem was that despite the new interest in mentoring, Glenn was now faced with carrying out a task for which there was little previous direction. Also, Dr. Ramirez wanted a plan for the program on his desk as soon as possible.

If you were assisting Glenn, what suggestions would you make for dealing with this assigned task?

_____

_____

_____

_____

_____

_____

One of the first things that could be done to make the Shadyville mentoring program an effective venture would be to realize that Glenn cannot do the task all by himself. He might be able to coordinate a program once it is off the ground, but the first thing that should occur is to bring together a planning team to work with Glenn on his assigned task. The mentoring planning team might consist of the district personnel director, the district curriculum coordinator or coordinator of staff development (if the district maintains these roles), principals and other administrators who will serve as mentors or who will be mentored, and perhaps representatives from the local community. If you were asked to put together a committee in your district that would be responsible for planning a mentoring program for school administrators, who would you include as members?

_____

_____

_____

_____

_____

_____

The composition of the Mentoring Planning Team must be unique to each school district and should be based on local concerns, conditions, and realities.

Mentoring Planning Team: Setting the Stage

Before you set up a mentoring program for the first time in a school district, outline the main components of the plan (its definition, purpose, and goals). Once your district has decided to adopt a mentoring program as a way to promote effective professional development for your administrative team, it needs to develop an implementation plan. Your plan might address the broad categories of issues that are noted in the following overview outline. Additional information regarding the various points is explained in subsequent chapters.

   I. Definition

    A. Are the terms used in the implementation plan clearly defined?

    B. Are the terms defined consistently throughout the plan?

   II. Purpose, rationale, or philosophy

    A. Is there a statement of purpose for the plan?

    B. Is the purpose compatible with the following:

        1. The school board's philosophy of education

        2. The professional development plan for the district

    C. Are the fundamental reasons for the adoption of a mentoring program stated?

    D. Does the rationale include statements of belief concerning areas that are related to mentoring?

        1. Does each statement of belief have a rational basis?

        2. Are the statements of belief compatible with each other?

    E. Does the rationale include specific implications of stated beliefs for mentoring?

        1. Do the specific implications flow logically from the general belief?

        2. Are the implications compatible with each other?

    F. Is the rationale compatible with the following:

        1. State or national trends

        2. The school board's general philosophy of education or expected outcomes

   III. Goals and objectives

    A. Are broad program goals written?

    B. Are program goals appropriately related to the stated needs?

    C. Are specific objectives written for each goal?

    D. Are the goals and objectives compatible with the following:

        1. Each other

        2. The school board's philosophy of education

3. Goals and objectives of other components of the district's professional development program

4. The purpose and rationale of the mentoring program

E. Does the plan include provisions for revising, adding, or deleting program objectives as a result of needs assessments that are administered to mentors and to all administrators?

F. Does the plan include provisions for mentors and all other administrators to set individual objectives?

Perhaps you have other questions that are relative to your local school system. Use the following space to list any of these additional issues that need to be addressed as you go about the initial planning for a mentoring program. (For example, a growing number of states now have legislation that requires mentoring for new principals. This legislation can mandate additional practices to be followed at the local district level.)

Implementation: Putting It All Together

After the stage has been set, you can begin the implementation process. Some of the major issues that need to be addressed at this point are (a) mentor selection, (b) mentor training, (c) mentor assignment, (d) matching system roles and responsibilities, and (e) target groups. The following outline gives an overview of these issues:

IV. Mentor selection

A. Are eligibility requirements for becoming a mentor stated?

B. Are procedures for nominating mentors stated?

C. Are criteria for selecting mentors stated?

D. Are all elements of the mentor selection process compatible with the following:

1. The overall purposes of the mentoring program

2. The rationale of the mentoring program

3. The goals and objectives of the mentoring program

V. Mentor training

A. Is orientation planned for the mentors?

1. Are goals and objectives for mentor orientation listed?

    2. Is there a tentative schedule of activities for mentor orientation?

    3. Does the plan for mentor orientation include making mentors aware of the following:

       a. Their roles and responsibilities

       b. Mentor training activities in which they will participate

       c. Support, rewards, and incentives for mentors

       d. The district's procedures for evaluating mentor performance

B. Is there a plan to have preliminary training for new mentors following mentor orientation and prior to the initiation of mentoring?

    1. Are the goals and objectives for preliminary mentor training listed?

    2. Is there a schedule of activities for preliminary mentor training?

    3. Do goals, objectives, and activities in the preliminary mentor training plan focus on knowledge and skills that will be needed by mentors during the first few weeks of mentoring?

C. Is there a plan for long-term mentor training?

    1. Are goals and objectives for long-term mentor training listed?

    2. Is there a schedule of activities for long-term mentor training?

D. Are there plans for mentor orientation, preliminary training for new mentors, and long-term mentor training based on the development of a preliminary needs assessment?

E. Are all elements of the plan for mentor training consistent with the following:

    1. The purpose of the overall program of professional development in your district

    2. The rationale, goals, and objectives of your district's plan for administrative professional development

F. Are human resources identified to coordinate and implement each planned mentor training activity?

G. Are material resources identified that are necessary to carry out mentor training?

VI. Mentor assignment and matching

A. Are there criteria established for assigning mentors?

    1. Are the criteria compatible with the knowledge base of matching mentors and protégés?

2. Do the criteria reflect practical considerations of the program size, types, and numbers of potential mentors?

B. Is there a description of the procedures for matching mentors and protégés?

    1. Are the procedures compatible with the knowledge base related to mentor matching?

    2. Do the procedures address the concerns of those who are directly affected by the mentor assignment?

    3. Is the issue of reassignment of mentors during the school year addressed?

C. Are criteria and procedures for matching mentors and protégés compatible with the following:

    1. The overall purposes of administrative professional development in the district

    2. The rationale, goals, and objectives of your district's professional development program

VII. System roles and responsibilities and mentor support

A. Are program responsibilities of your school district's central office, responsibilities at the building level, and responsibilities of other organizations that are involved in the mentoring program clearly defined and delineated?

B. Are the roles and responsibilities of all people who are involved in the mentoring program clearly defined?

C. Support and rewards

    1. Are provisions made for regular group meetings that focus on support for mentors?

    2. Is a support person identified to coordinate the activities of mentors?

    3. Are mentors provided with sufficient time to carry out their responsibilities?

    4. Are provisions made for mentors to receive resources that are essential for carrying out their mentoring responsibilities?

D. Rewards and mentors

    1. Are there extrinsic rewards for mentors (such as financial rewards or additional release time)?

    2. Are there provisions for school district recognition of particularly effective mentors?

3. Are there incentives for mentors to engage in individualized activities in order to promote their personal and professional development?

E. Are all elements of the plan for providing support and rewards for mentors compatible with the following:

1. The purposes of your district's professional development program

2. The rationale, goals, and objectives of your district's professional development program

F. Are human resources identified in order to coordinate support and rewards for mentors?

G. Are material resources identified that are necessary to provide support and rewards for mentors?

VIII. Identifying appropriate target groups

A. Will your mentoring program be directed exclusively at the needs of beginning school administrators in your district? Or, will it be available to all administrators?

B. Is there a clear understanding of the kinds of issues that need to be included in mentoring programs for beginning administrators (as opposed to topics that are more appropriate for veterans)?

List any additional questions that you believe need to be answered as you begin to implement your program.

_____

_____

_____

_____

_____

_____

Appraisal: How Did It Work?

Finally, the mentoring planning team needs to consider a variety of questions that are designed to help determine whether the mentoring program achieved its goals and objectives, whether the implementation process seemed to be successful, and whether changes might be needed for the initial program design or implementation plan.

IX. Program evaluation and revision

   A. Phases of program evaluation

      1. Context evaluation

         a. Is there a plan for identifying environmental factors that might affect your mentoring program or its outcomes?

         b. Does the plan include methods for measuring the effects of these factors on the mentoring program and its outcomes?

         c. Are there provisions for determining whether the program-needs assessment has correctly identified the needs of mentors and of all district administrators?

      2. Input evaluation

         a. Are there provisions for evaluating your written program?

         b. Are there provisions for evaluating the appropriateness and adequacy of human and material resources that are assigned to the mentoring program?

      3. Process evaluation

         a. Are there provisions for determining whether the mentoring program has been implemented according to your stated program goals?

         b. If any components of the mentoring program have not been implemented according to your plan, are there provisions for identifying the lack of implementation?

         c. Are there provisions for identifying the effects of the lack of implementation?

      4. Outcomes evaluation

         a. Is there a plan to measure whether or not the program objectives have been met?

         b. Is there a plan to measure positive, negative, and unintended program outcomes?

      5. Are there provisions for analyzing data from each phase of the program evaluation and for synthesizing the results of that analysis in a comprehensive evaluation report?

   B. Are there procedures for revising the mentoring program in response to the program evaluation?

   C. Are human resources identified in order to coordinate and implement program evaluation and revision?

      D. Are material resources identified that are necessary for program evaluation?

   X. Needs assessment for program modifications

      A. Mentors

          1. Are provisions made for formal and informal ongoing needs assessments?

          2. Are provisions made for modifying mentor training or mentor support as a result of the mentor needs assessment that is administered during the first year of implementation?

      B. Are human resources identified in order to coordinate and implement mentor needs assessment and corresponding modifications in the mentoring program?

      C. Are material resources identified that are necessary to carry out mentor needs assessment?

What are some of the other questions that you believe will need to be answered as part of a comprehensive evaluation of the mentoring program that is being implemented in your district?

Summarizing the Chapter

These questions are meant to assist you as you begin to formulate a local approach to an effective mentoring program that can be used to assist with the professional development of school administrators in your district. Simply responding to the questions, however, will not create the plan. Instead, you must look at your own local district priorities and conditions in order to determine appropriate strategies to be used in developing an effective program.

In addition to the other issues that are raised in this chapter, it would be helpful to think of the following conditions that need to be addressed as part of the implementation process for a mentoring program in any district:

- Commitment on the part of the central office and the school board is critical.
- School board policy that is supportive of the program is important.
- A local mentoring planning team should be created.
- A budget must be planned.
- Requisite human and resource materials need to be identified.
- The program structure should be designed.
- Goals and objectives are necessary.
- The implementation plan should be specified.
- Evaluation processes need to be identified before the program actually gets underway.

3

What Is Our Purpose?

THERE IS LITTLE DOUBT that the most important part of any planning process is the identification of the primary purposes behind the activity. This chapter considers some of the possible goals, objectives, and purposes that you might propose as you set up a framework for the implementation of your local mentoring program for school leaders. Again, you must take sufficient time to decide precisely why you want to have mentoring in your school system and which philosophy will guide your actions.

Decide the Target Groups

Structured mentoring programs can be used to serve as part of the professional development process for two main groups of school administrators: beginners and veterans. When planning your program, you should decide early who will be the target of your effort. Whichever local vision or definition of mentoring you adopt, what will serve as the foundation for any mentoring program is the fact that this activity needs to be understood as part of a true developmental relationship that is tied to an appreciation of life and career stages. Unfortunately, most discussions of mentoring in education have not taken this perspective. The term *mentor* has traditionally been defined as anyone who is able to demonstrate craft knowledge to a beginner.

The assumption that you need to make when designing an effective mentoring program for administrators is that the role of the mentor will be different depending on the level of professional experience of practicing administrators. In other words, mentoring for beginning principals is not the same as mentoring for experienced administrators. Mentoring for those who have first stepped into the field of administration as assistant principals or principals is different from the kind of support that is called for by experienced school administrators who are first walking into a central office position or superintendency. Most importantly, mentoring implies a professional activity and commitment that goes well beyond simply being able to answer questions about "the way they do things around here."

As you plan for an effective mentoring program, consider the following possible different groups for whom your program might be designed:

- *Inexperienced, Beginning Administrators*—These are individuals who are taking their first jobs in administration. In most cases, these people have the roles of assistant principal or principal and have come directly from the classroom or from some other non-administrative role (such as a counselor). These are the true rookies.

- *Experienced Administrators Who Are New to Your District*—In many districts, there is an expectation that individuals who are hired for principalships or other administrative roles have previous experience as school administrators. What that usually implies is that the district has an unstated policy of going outside to find new leaders. Unfortunately, many districts assume that because a person has a good deal of experience in another system, he or she will be able to step into a new district and will be able to perform effectively without any guidance or support. Clearly, such an assumption is not valid. Anyone who is new to an organization needs assistance when it comes to learning about local norms, policies, and issues. As a result, a mentoring program for experienced principals or other administrators who are new to your district is a valuable activity.

- *Veterans*—These are the administrators who have more than a few years of experience with working in your school system. The typical assumption is that because they have been in the organization for a while, they need no special guidance or assistance to help them do their jobs. In fact, the public norms of many school systems indicate that any experienced administrator who admits that he or she needs help is an ineffective administrator. Again, the Lone Ranger vision of school administration is alive and well (and is unfortunate indeed).

  Mentoring can be an important form of support for any school administrator. A paradox can often be heard in discussions related to this group, however. Chapter 4, "Who Is a Mentor?" includes characteristics of effective mentors and shows that they have had successful experiences in their roles. As a result, mentors will be drawn from the category of experienced veterans. What this situation implies is that your district might wish to consider developing mentors to assist mentors.

Such a vision means that mentoring must be something that is well beyond simply answering occasional questions about how to do the job.

- *Superintendents*—This focus would imply that mentoring must be viewed as something that takes place beyond the boundaries of an individual school system. As the chief executive officers of school systems, superintendents have no hierarchical peers in their own school district. As a result, mentors are most likely individuals who come from other school districts. This situation will be a difficult kind of arrangement to develop (given the traditionally competitive nature of school districts and their leaders). Nevertheless, it is obvious that the superintendency is filled with the pressures that make it critical for people to receive some form of ongoing support. That statement is equally true of beginning superintendents and their experienced colleagues.

As you begin the process of planning for a mentoring program in your district, which of these groups will serve as the focus of your efforts?

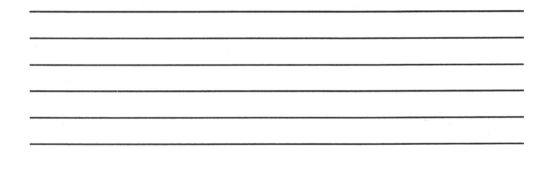

Two Cases

Roberto Garcia spent 15 years as an elementary school teacher in the Green Acres local schools. He was generally regarded as one of the district's most effective elementary teachers, and many administrators in the system often encouraged him to think about a future as a principal. With that support, he enrolled in graduate courses in educational leadership at State University, and soon he was certified as an elementary principal. In a short time, he received his first assignment as a building administrator in the Green Acres school district.

Roberto was extremely happy to receive word that his assignment would be at Sherman School. He had worked there for nine years, so he knew quite a few of the teachers. He knew the neighborhood where the school was located, and he was aware of a lot of the issues that would likely face him as a principal. Despite these facts, he quickly realized that he really did not have as good a handle on how to be an effective leader for Sherman as he had once believed.

One of the things that he realized was that the teachers, many of whom he had known for several years, looked at him very differently now that he was "the boss." As he walked into the teachers' lounge one day, he suddenly noticed that all conversations either ceased or at least shifted in tone. In the past, he had been the life of the party in many lounge conversations. As a teacher, he was always telling jokes, sharing gossip, and being the center of attention. As the principal, he recognized that his presence had created a chilling effect on the tone of the group. In short, he felt as if the group with whom he used to talk openly was now talking about him.

Roberto also rather quickly became aware of the amount of paperwork that he had to do and deadlines that he had to meet as a principal. Back at State University, the professors told him that principals were responsible for things such as parent and community relations, communication with the central office, building budget oversight, scheduling, staff and teacher appraisal, and so on. It all sounded so doable when he was sitting in the back of Dr. Crooks' class on school law. Now, he suddenly realized that the court cases he had to memorize did not have much to do with what it was like to be a principal. He now often felt overwhelmed by the tasks and the overall job. If only he had someone to help him through his set of tasks. Getting an A from Dr. Crooks had little relevance to his world now.

In another school district not too far from Roberto's, we find Rachel Gilcrest, a middle school principal in her ninth year of service as a building administrator. She always appeared to be totally happy with her job, and she had had no problems with her responsibilities as a school principal. All of her colleagues in her district looked up to her as one of the strongest instructional leaders in the system. Everything was perfect in her professional life (or so it seemed to anyone who looked at her life for a moment).

People who really knew Rachel understood that she was not as happy as she appeared. For example, because she was the only principal in her district with a Ph.D., she was often asked to serve on committees and present in-service sessions in her district for teachers and for her colleague administrators. These demands on her personal time were not the only things that frustrated her. She was also the only woman principal who was currently working in the system, so she was often called upon to partake in a variety of community forums in which it was critical for the district to appear balanced in terms of gender representation. In short, Rachel was getting worn out by all of the demands placed on her.

In addition to the many time constraints that she felt, Rachel was also becoming increasingly frustrated with her work as a principal. She had gotten into this business to bring about necessary changes in school practices. Nine years later, she still felt that she was doing little more than keeping the ship afloat. Despite many positive signs from her teachers and parents, she often did not feel that she was an instructional leader at all.

In cases such as these, having a mentoring program for administrators would be helpful (whether the principal is a beginner, like Roberto, or is a more experienced individual, such as Rachel).

In what ways do you believe that a mentoring program would be helpful to the two principals in these brief scenarios?

_____

_____

_____

_____

_____

_____

Identifying a Purpose

In addition to selecting the target group for your mentoring program, it is also critical to understand that there are multiple purposes toward which any effective mentoring program can be directed. It is important to identify the specific purposes for which your program will be developed; otherwise, the mentoring program that you design might consist of little more than finding a few administrators to answer questions from time to time. That would be fatal to the long-term health and well being of your program.

Basically, most school districts want a mentoring program for two reasons:

1. **Career advancement**—This advancement involves mentoring that stresses the grasping of technical survival skills that individuals need so that they can get and keep a job.

2. **Psychosocial development**—This approach to mentoring stresses a holistic approach to adult learning and encourages individuals to grow professionally as well as personally.

Neither of these purposes is wrong or incomplete. It is perfectly reasonable to develop a mentoring system that focuses exclusively on promoting career advancement, for example. Most mentoring programs that are designed for use in private corporations tend to focus primarily on providing career advancement support for protégés. For example, great effort is put into helping employees discover the ways to survive in the company and to move up the corporate ladder.

In schools, the notion of helping people move up is not as relevant as it is in most private corporations (where there are multiple opportunities to advance in terms of prestige, position, and pay). Schools tend to be relatively flat organizations with only a few possible levels of advancement, and increasingly, people are not necessarily looking at the principalship as a promotion from teaching. Furthermore, the superintendency long ago lost its luster as a promotion beyond the principalship.

Nevertheless, the concept of career advancement has a value in education—particularly if the focus is on helping people survive their first few years of professional service.

By contrast, most private corporation mentoring schemes pay little attention to psychosocial development as a focus and purpose. In educational administration, this purpose becomes much more appropriate and likely. Research on the life of administrators—whether they are at the beginning of their careers or are well experienced—shows consistently that the life of the school leader is often lonely, frustrating, and full of interpersonal conflict. As a result, the need for someone to provide for the school administrator's psychosocial development is clear.

As you develop your mentoring program for school administrators in your district, what will be the primary focus of your program?

_____

_____

_____

_____

_____

_____

Administrators: A Special Case

Currently, many school systems have mentoring programs in place that are designed to assist beginning classroom teachers, and there is a tendency to simply apply the same practices and structures to administrative personnel. Such a practice is a mistake. Administrators are a special case, and they deserve their own program of professional development.

Some of the ways in which administrators are different from teachers include the following:

1. **The research base on administration is not clear enough to guide mentoring programs**—There is relatively little research that specifically describes the nature of behaviors of effective administrators. Although this knowledge base is growing, it is not even close to what is now found in the area of teacher education. Without an equivalent research base, it is hard to lead people through mentoring relationships.

2. **Administrators do their jobs in isolation from peers**—Mentoring programs for teachers assume that these educators have access to many colleagues each day who can provide feedback regarding job performance. There are many teachers in a building. In contrast, there is usually no other administrator on duty with a principal (particularly in an elementary school). This situation results in administrators having different needs for ongoing support because they work apart from their administrative colleagues.

3. **New administrators are not new to schools**—In most states, there is an expectation that administrators will have teaching experience before taking their first managerial jobs. This expectation does nothing to ensure that the administrator is completely sensitive to the demands of his or her new job. On the other hand, the beginning principal at least knows what a school looks like, knows how students tend to behave, and knows what parents are likely to ask for or demand. In a mentoring program for administrators, there is less demand for an initial orientation to the world of schools and professional education.

4. **Administrators are bosses**—When people receive administrative assignments, they automatically take on positions of legal and formal power, authority, and control. A school administrator, even on the first day on the job, is a boss who has been appointed by a local governing body to manage a part of the school district's programs and facilities. This position makes it somewhat difficult to design programs of support, whether for the entry year on the job or even later in the administrator's career.

5. **Administrative peers are usually not true equals to the beginner**—Administrators face the need to understand the pecking order among the administrative personnel in their systems. Although all principals appear to be the same on the organizational chart, the fact is that some have greater influence than others. Mentoring programs that assume that all administrators are equal deny the reality of organizational life found in school systems.

Does your school system currently have a mentoring program to assist classroom teachers?

_____

_____

If so, does this list relate to ways in which you would have to modify your current mentoring program for teachers in order to make it more appropriate for school administrators? If so, how? (For example, how do you provide for principals leaving their buildings during the day to visit their mentors or protégés? In teacher programs, mentors are typically in the same schools with their protégés.)

_____

_____

_____

_____

_____

_____

Checking Your Plan

Refer to the questions that were asked in Chapter 2, "Initial Program Development," to help you design a plan for your mentoring program. Note that many of the individual items refer specifically to issues that are addressed in this chapter. Use the following checklist to assist you with reviewing important basic planning issues, and modify your plan if necessary.

A. Is there a statement of purpose for your implementation plan?

    1. The school board's philosophy of education

    ____ Yes   ____ No

B. Is the purpose compatible with the following:

    1. The school board's philosophy of education

    ____ Yes   ____ No

    2. The professional development plan for the district

    ____ Yes   ____ No

C. Are the fundamental reasons for the adoption of a mentoring program stated?

_____ Yes _____ No

D. Does the rationale include statements of belief concerning areas that are relative to mentoring as a form of administrative support?

_____ Yes _____ No

1. Does each statement of belief have a rational basis?

_____ Yes _____ No

2. Are the statements of belief compatible with each other?

_____ Yes _____ No

E. Does the rationale include specific implications of stated beliefs for mentoring?

_____ Yes _____ No

1. Do the specific implications flow logically from the general belief?

_____ Yes _____ No

2. Are the implications compatible with each other?

_____ Yes _____ No

F. Is the rationale compatible with the following:

1. State or national trends

_____ Yes _____ No

2. The school board's general philosophy of education or expected outcomes

_____ Yes _____ No

G. Are broad program goals written?

_____ Yes _____ No

H. Are the program goals appropriate for the stated needs?

_____ Yes _____ No

I. Are specific objectives written for each goal?

_____ Yes _____ No

J. Are the goals and objectives compatible with the following:

1. Each other

_____ Yes _____ No

2. The school board's philosophy of education

_____ Yes _____ No

3. Goals and objectives of other components of the district's professional development program

_____ Yes _____ No

4. The purpose and rationale of the mentoring program

_____ Yes _____ No

K. Does the plan include provisions for revising, adding, or deleting program objectives as a result of needs assessments that are administered to mentors and all administrators?

_____ Yes _____ No

L. Does the plan include provisions for mentors and all other administrators to set individual objectives?

_____ Yes _____ No

Summarizing the Chapter

This chapter considered the importance of understanding the purpose of a mentoring program before you actually begin to implement it in your district. Emphasis was placed upon the following points:

- Mentoring programs can be designed for beginner or veteran school administrators. You must decide which group is your focus or whether you wish to support both groups.

- Mentoring programs can focus on career advancement, psychosocial development, or both.

- Mentoring programs for teachers are not sufficient to deal with the complex issues that school administrators face.

PART II

Implementing Your Program

THE MILTON SCHOOLS were extremely proud of their reputation as a school district that was on the cutting edge of school improvement and innovation. Each year, Milton students were at or near the top of lists showing statewide performance on standardized tests. Not only did the district shine as a lighthouse when it came to student performance, but it was also regarded as a national model for commitment to staff development.

One of the greatest accomplishments in the district was the recent decision to initiate a mentoring program for administrators in the district. With the title of Leaders for the Future, the program had received a lot of positive publicity. The district planned to demonstrate its vision of *total quality management* (TQM) by making certain that its administrative team would now get the same opportunities for learning and development that were always available to Milton teachers. Because the students in the district always achieved well, it was clear that the teachers had gained much from their staff development. Now, it would be the administrators' turn to learn and grow. The slogan adopted by the district was "Milton leaders will help Milton leaders who will help your children learn." Dr. Martin Gimble, executive director of human resource development for the district, was named as the person in charge of the new mentoring program. He had already followed good practice by calling together a mentoring planning team that consisted of representatives across the school system. The team had developed its own working definitions for the new program, along with a clear identification of its goals, objectives, and limitations. Team members decided that mentoring would be not only for new administrators; all administrators in the central office and also in the schools around the system would have mentors for the next year. They also agreed to develop the new program without direct reference to the district's highly regarded mentoring effort for classroom teachers (an activity that had received national visibility over the past three years).

The mentoring planning team worked carefully on all of the needed planning issues for most of a school year. Now it was April, and the expectation was that the mentoring program would go online in August. It was time to set in motion a way to make the slogans become reality.

Work with school systems across the country has shown that the case of the Milton Schools is not typical. Most districts, unfortunately, do not engage in the type of systematic development that is shown in this scenario. More often than not, the idea to start a mentoring program comes in late spring, with the expectation that it will start immediately or in only a month or two.

Because the reality is that districts engage in simultaneous planning and implementation of many projects, the chapters in Part II include a number of issues that should help you and other members of the your local planning team as you initiate your district program. You will find issues that are associated with the identification of mentors, training, specific suggestions for mentor practice, and possible curricula for mentoring programs that are directed toward the needs of both beginning and veteran school leaders.

4

Who Is a Mentor?

ONCE THE MENTORING PLANNING TEAM has considered the basic structure of the program, it is important for them to proceed with the implementation process. The most critical task involves determining what the mentoring program in your district should look like. This determination will automatically lead you to making a decision about another important issue—namely, who your mentors will be and what their specific responsibilities will be in meeting the challenges of your local program's definition.

In this chapter, you will find (a) information to help you decide who should and should not serve as mentors, (b) information about how to identify the ideal characteristics of mentors, and (c) information about a number of responsibilities for administrative mentors.

Characteristics of Mentors: One Case

Sally Halsted has been a principal in the Garden City School District for 18 years. She has been perceived as a strong administrator throughout her career. Two years ago, she was named Principal of the Year for her state. When the mentoring planning team for Garden City was trying to identify good principals to serve as mentors for the new principals in the district, Sally was at the top of the list. Surely, a principal with her skill was exactly the kind of individual that should serve as a role model and mentor for the newcomers in the district.

During the following school year, the mentoring program for new principals in Garden City was started. Sally was assigned to work with her first protégé, Ed Dinkle—a bright young man who had recently been named to serve as the administrator of the West End Elementary School. Ed had come to Garden City after several years of effective teaching in a neighboring district. This principalship was his first.

At first, the relationship between Ed and Sally seemed to be very positive. They had weekly meetings concerning the kinds of matters that often trouble beginning principals (how to start the school year, who the key people are in the central office, and so forth). After about six weeks, however, the partnership between Ed and Sally seemed to change drastically. Ed was frustrated because Sally always appeared to be so busy with her own duties and commitments to the state principals' association that she was rarely available when Ed had an important question. The other difficulty that was making Ed uncomfortable was the way that she responded to his questions. Whenever he finally got in touch with Sally, she did little more than respond by saying, "If I were you, I'd . . . " On more than a few occasions, Ed felt as if Sally was simply giving him answers so that he would not bother her anymore.

Sally continued to enjoy being called a mentor, particularly to a bright newcomer such as Ed. She knew that Ed was making a few mistakes here and there, but she was extremely proud to note that no one at the central office had learned about any of his miscues. She was always able to make the right calls and fix Ed's mistakes before he got into any serious trouble with "downtown."

After reading this brief case study, would you consider Sally to be an effective administrative mentor?

_____

_____

What are some of the positive characteristics that would contribute to Sally's ability to serve as an effective mentor?

_____

_____

What are some of the negative characteristics that would suggest that she would be a bad selection as a mentor in the future?

_____

_____

Now that Sally has been identified as a mentor who has some problems, what could the mentoring planning team suggest to her as a way to improve her performance in the future?

_____

_____

_____

_____

_____

_____

Characteristics of Mentors: A Second Case

Jack Laskowski achieved a major personal and professional goal a few weeks ago when he became the principal of the Rolling Meadow Primary School. He was quite proud of his accomplishment and looked forward to serving his new community. He was confident that he could do the job.

One of the main reasons for Jack's confidence was the fact that as a new principal, he would have at least one person in his district who would be able to help him negotiate the rough spots that he was sure to face. Within days after getting the word that he would be the principal of Rolling Meadow, he received word that his mentor would be Janet Tortorelli, another elementary principal who had about 10 years of experience as an administrator in the district. Janet came over to visit Jack soon after her phone call. She spent a lot of time learning about his background, his personal goals, and the vision that he had for his school. During that session, she said little and listened very carefully to Jack. At the end of that first meeting, Janet and Jack worked out a plan that included a tentative schedule of visits to each other's buildings and times for periodic meetings during the next year.

Jack felt ready to take on the challenges of the principalship. A big part of that feeling of readiness came about because of his mentor.

After reading this scenario, do you believe that Janet is likely to serve as an effective mentor?

_____

_____

What are some of Janet's positive characteristics?

_____

_____

_____

_____

_____

_____

Do you have someone who is ready to step in to serve as a mentor (as Janet has done for Jack)?

_____

_____

_____

_____

_____

_____

Are Effective Principals Always Good Mentors?

Research has shown that good administrative mentors must be good principals but that good principals do not always serve as good mentors. Being an effective mentor requires a variety of skills and abilities that go beyond those that are required for leading a school's staff.

All good principals can be effective and help their colleagues in a school district in a number of ways:

- **As peer pals**—Individuals who are at the same level as colleagues can share job-related information, strategies, and support for mutual benefit.

- **As career guides**—People who are not necessarily in positions in which they can champion or protect their colleagues can explain the system to others.

- **As sponsors**—Individuals who do not necessarily have organizational power can still promote and shape colleagues' careers.

- **As patrons**—Influential people can use their own power to help advance other people's careers.

All of these helping roles are important. None is the same as being a true mentor, however—an individual who assumes the role of both teacher and advocate as part of an intensive, continuing, and mutually enhancing relationship. The key here is that mentors can engage in the same helping behaviors as peer pals, career guides, and so forth. They go beyond these roles, however, and demonstrate characteristics that are even more focused on the needs of the individuals with whom they are working.

Think back on your own career and reflect on people who served in the capacity of each of the helping roles listed here:

Peer pal: _____

Career guide: _____

Sponsor: _____

Patron: _____

Now, consider one or more people that you have known who were more like the definition of a true mentor. List a few of these individuals with whom you have had contact during your professional life, and write down some of the characteristics that they demonstrated to you that made them effective mentors.

_____

_____

What Are Some Characteristics of Effective Mentors?

A number of desirable characteristics are listed here to aid you in selecting mentors for school administrators:

1. Mentors should have experience as practicing school administrators, and their peers and others should generally regard them as being effective.

2. Mentors must demonstrate generally accepted positive leadership qualities such as, but not limited to, the following:

   a. Intelligence

   b. Good oral and written communication skills

   c. A capacity to understand the messages of the past as a guide

   d. Acceptance of multiple alternative solutions to complex problems

   e. Clarity of vision and the ability to share that vision with others in the organization

3. Mentors ask the right questions of beginning administrators and not just providing the right answers all the time

4. Mentors must accept an alternate way of doing things and should avoid the tendency to tell beginners that the way to do something is "the way that I used to do it."

5. Mentors should express the desire to see people go beyond their present levels of performance, even if it might mean that the protégés are able to do some things better than the mentors can.

6. Mentors need to model the principles of continuous learning and reflection.

7. Mentors must exhibit the awareness of the political and social realities of life in at least one school system; they must know the "real ways" in which things get done.

Compare this list with the characteristics of mentors you have known. Add any additional skills that you included in your review:

_____

_____

_____

_____

In addition to these characteristics, other skills and abilities are often used to describe ideal mentors. Typically, these individuals demonstrate the following:

- Knowledge, skills, and expertise in a particular field of practice
- Enthusiasm that is sincere and convincing—and, most importantly, the ability to convey this feeling to those whom they are mentoring
- The ability to communicate to others a clear picture of personal attitudes, values, and ethical standards
- The ability to communicate in a sensitive way the type of feedback that is needed regarding another person's progress toward desirable goals, standards, competence, and professional behavior
- The ability to listen to colleagues' ideas, doubts, concerns, and questions
- A caring attitude and a belief in their colleagues' potential flexibility and sense of humor

These criteria are helpful in the selection process. Before selection, however, you must recruit individuals to become involved with your mentoring program. Five important skills need to be shown by those who are to serve in an administrative mentoring program:

1. They must have a willingness to invest time and energy in the professional development of their colleagues.

2. They must have a strong conviction and belief that other administrators are likely to have a positive effect on the quality of schooling.

3. They must have confidence in their own abilities.

4. They must possess high standards and expectations for their own abilities and for the work of their colleagues.

5. They must believe that mentoring is a mutually enhancing professional development opportunity in which both partners will achieve equal satisfaction from the relationship.

Danger Signals

The following characteristics signal individuals who probably should not serve as mentors:

1. Persons who are too heavily involved with the internal politics of a school system will be ineffective mentors. Often, their primary goals are to simply survive or enhance their personal status in the system. (It is important for newcomers to understand the political realities of a system. It is not important for a person to learn how to spend most of her or his time jockeying for a position.)

2. An individual who is new to a position will be ineffective in a relationship with another novice. (For example, experienced principals who are in their first year in the central office frequently have so many things to learn that they might need a mentor themselves and might not have sufficient time to spend with a beginning principal.)

3. A marginally effective administrator should not be selected to serve as a mentor on the basis that such an assignment would serve to "fix" his or her shortcomings. (Although it is true that service as a mentor can increase an administrator's effectiveness, it does not make good sense to match a beginner with anyone who is not able to demonstrate the very best behavior that is associated with an effective educational leader.)

4. Ineffective mentors demonstrate know-it-all behaviors and attitudes when discussing their ways of dealing with administrative problems. Clearly, self-confidence is desirable in a mentor. Being closed-minded about alternative solutions for complex problems, however, is probably a mark of a person's insecurity.

What might be some other danger signals of administrators who might not be very effective in the mentor role?

_____

_____

_____

_____

Responsibilities of Mentors

Now that you have reviewed some of the characteristics of effective and ineffective mentors for school administrators, let's look at some of their major duties and responsibilities:

- To give their time to others
- To listen and sympathize with colleagues without necessarily condoning or condemning what might at times seem to be inappropriate or ineffective actions
- To manifest a sense of humor but to avoid sarcasm and cynicism
- To appreciate that good leaders are sometimes not able to play the role of effective mentors, but that effective mentors must always be good leaders

Another way of viewing the functions and duties of mentors is as follows:

- *Advising:* The mentor responds to a colleague's need to gain the information that is needed to carry out a job effectively.
- *Communicating:* The mentor works consistently in order to ensure that open lines of communication are always available.
- *Counseling:* The mentor provides needed emotional support to a colleague.
- *Guiding:* The mentor works to acquaint a new colleague with the informal and formal norms of a particular system.

- *Modeling:* The mentor serves as a role model by consistently demonstrating professional and competent performance on the job.

- *Protecting:* When needed, the mentor serves as a buffer between a colleague and those in the system who might wish to detract from that person's performance.

- *Skill Developing:* The mentor assists others with learning skills that are needed to carry out their jobs effectively.

Checking Your Plan

To guide your planning, refer to the list in Chapter 2, "Initial Program Development." Check to see how well you have addressed each of the following items that deal with mentor recruitment and selection:

A. Are eligibility requirements for becoming a mentor stated?

_____ Yes _____ No

B. Are procedures for nominating mentors stated?

_____ Yes _____ No

C. Are criteria for selecting mentors stated?

_____ Yes _____ No

D. Are all elements of the mentor selection process compatible with the following:

1. The overall purposes of the mentoring program

_____ Yes _____ No

2. The rationale of the mentoring program

_____ Yes _____ No

3. The goals and objectives of the mentoring program

_____ Yes _____ No

Summarizing the Chapter

This chapter considered the critical issue of deciding who will serve as mentors in your program. There are no magic recipes to ensure that everyone who is designated as a mentor will be effective in that role. It takes more than a long record as an administrator and recognition as a strong leader to make someone a good mentor. It must be a spirit that comes from within special people.

5

Preparing People to Serve as Mentors

THERE ARE THOSE WHO SAY that the ability to serve as a mentor is a special gift. As a result, the whole notion of trying to prepare individuals to mentor others is impossible, they would say. You either have the talent or you do not.

Mentoring is indeed a talent, and some people have natural skills that are related to providing support and guidance to others. In addition, many people possess great talent as mentors but have never been called upon to use those talents. Some individuals, however, might be able to acquire many of the skills that are associated with effective mentoring—even if they are not naturally gifted as mentors. For these reasons, it is possible to suggest learning activities that will assist people with becoming more effective mentors to their administrative protégés.

This chapter describes a model that can be used to prepare individuals as mentors in programs that are designed to support aspiring and practicing school administrators. There are five domains in the model, and for each domain, specific training activities are described. The model has been used extensively with local school districts, universities, and state education agencies.

Domain 1: Orientation to Mentoring

Here, the primary goal is to develop a consensus definition of what mentoring is, what some of its benefits are, some problems that are traditionally associated with mentoring programs, and so forth. This description is an expansion of much of the material that was presented in Chapter 1 ("What Is Mentoring, and Why Is It So Important?") and in other sections of this book. Devoting time to a general orientation of what mentoring is (and what it is not) for school leaders is worthwhile for several reasons. First, the word *mentoring* has been so widely used to denote such a wide array of relationships that it has started to lose much of its real value. People frequently talk about mentors they have had, only revealing that these mentors range from people who were available to "show new folks around the office" to the kinds of thoughtful individuals who engage in mutually enhancing relationships (as promoted in this book). Finding a common definition of mentoring is an important first step in this vision of professional development for school leaders.

It is often easier to explain true mentorship by identifying real-life examples that are found in the lives of participants. If you were to identify individuals in your personal or professional life who have made a difference by helping you become the best that you could be, who would they be? (List the names of mentors whom you have had in the past.)

_____

_____

_____

_____

_____

_____

Based on your recollection of what these various individuals did to help you, what might your personal definition of mentoring be?

_____

_____

_____

_____

Discussions during training sessions can include many examples of real mentoring that have occurred in the lives of successful leaders. People talk frequently about a particular teacher from their high school days, a pastor, a spouse, or any one of hundreds of others who were influential in their lives. Principals recall their days as assistant principals, when they walked at the side of an experienced administrator who pointed to certain talents and strengths of their colleagues. All of these stories are important in helping people appreciate the concept and value of mentoring.

Domain 2: Instructional Leadership

The next part of training for mentors involves a consideration of the question, "Mentoring for what?" This question deals with the important issue of helping people decide what the outcomes of a mentoring relationship should look like. It is important to decide what benefits might be derived by a school system if it invests time and money in order to carry out a mentoring program. Will administrators who have mentors become more effective as instructional leaders? What do effective instructional leaders look like?

In the following space, indicate some of the key characteristics that you believe should be displayed by principals and other school administrators who serve as instructional leaders rather than as mere building managers:

_____

_____

_____

_____

_____

_____

Some of the characteristics of effective instructional leaders that are shared during this point in the mentor training include the following:

1. Instructional leaders have a vision that is derived from their ongoing discussions with staff and other parties that have an interest in the school. (The leader is able to articulate what a school is supposed to do, particularly in terms of what it should do to benefit students.)

2. They make use of participative management techniques. They allow teachers and other staff members to participate meaningfully in real decision making and not merely in "playing at" getting people to be involved (when, in fact, decisions have already been made).

3. They view instruction as primary. (When tough decisions must be made about how to spend limited resources, the enhancement of instruction is always the highest priority to be supported in the school.)

4. They know what is going on in the classrooms of their schools. (They do not spend much time in their offices; they are out and about in their buildings and

spend a high percentage of their time in classes interacting with students and teachers.)

5. They find needed resources.

Another important issue to be included in this part of the training involves the sharing of personal visions, values, and philosophies of the mentors and administrators with whom they are working. Research on effective leadership shows clearly that leadership is based on one's ability to articulate one's own set of values that are clear and consistent with a philosophy espoused by the mentor.

Discussing personal philosophies of mentors and protégés might seem like a tedious activity, but it is not. As people articulate their values and visions for leadership, open and meaningful dialogue becomes much easier to achieve. It is suggested, therefore, that part of the time that is spent looking at instructional leadership should be devoted to helping people express some of their fundamental values related to education. Some of the questions that are suggested as a way to help people articulate their educational philosophies (or platforms) are as follows:

1. What do you hope to achieve in your school this year? How will you personally know when these goals are achieved?

2. How will students look after going through the next year in the school?

3. What will the teachers' roles be in achieving these goals? What will be the roles of students, parents, and other staff members?

4. What are some of the most important personal values you possess that cannot be violated? (What are the kinds of values that you hold before you start looking for another job?)

What are some additional questions that you believe would draw out a person's personal core educational values and beliefs?

_____

_____

_____

_____

_____

_____

Developing a personal philosophy or platform statement is a valuable activity. Sharing it with a mentor or protégé is even more powerful. This process can enable mentors to identify particular strengths of their protégés. In turn, this situation enables people to celebrate success—an activity that is not done frequently enough in most organizations.

Domain 3: Human Relations Skills

The process of mentoring requires considerable skill in the area of effective human relations. Again, training in this area does not pretend to make people who have no great interpersonal skill become perfect overnight. Training here can identify some areas in which people need greater awareness of key ideas if they are to work more effectively in the highly personalized world of effective mentoring, however.

Specifically, some information might be provided concerning adult learning and development and the importance of appreciating alternative behavioral styles. For the most part, people who serve as mentors have considerable experience working with children as learners, but they have had little training and appreciation for the unique learning of adults. Furthermore, because people display a wide array of alternative behavioral and learning styles, it is critical for those who would serve as effective mentors to appreciate this diversity by understanding alternative styles.

To illustrate the kinds of things that differentiate the learning patterns of adults, take a moment to respond to the following questions about the last time that you, as an adult, learned something. (It does not have to be some major learning event, like learning the theory of relativity. It can be something as simple as learning how to play a song on a piano or how to use new computer software.)

1. Why did you want to learn it?

_____

_____

_____

_____

2. How did you learn it?

_____

_____

_____

_____

3. To what *old* knowledge did the new learning connect?

_____

_____

_____

_____

4. What is the current status of the new learning?

_____

_____

_____

_____

_____

Your answers to these questions will likely parallel many of the following characteristics of effective adult learning that have been identified by researchers over the years:

Adults learn best when

- The learning activities in which they engage are viewed as realistic and are related to personal importance of the learner.

- What is to be learned is viewed as related to personal and professional goals.

- The learner can receive accurate feedback about personal progress toward the goals.

- The learner experiences success.

- The motivation to learn truly comes from within the individual learner.

In contrast, it is also known that adult learners often resist experiences when

- They feel as if the learning process becomes an attack on their personal or professional competence.

- They perceive that they are being given prescriptions for learning that oversimplify complex issues.

These concepts are introduced into mentor training because of the importance of mentors keeping a consistent image in their minds of the protégé as a colleague and an adult learner.

There are a number of different ways in which the concept of alternative behavioral patterns is introduced into mentor training. Most practicing administrators have participated in one or more exercises in which they have been placed into different behavioral categories, such as analyzer, controller, amiable, extrovert, task oriented, and so forth. If you have gone through one or more of these exercises during some point in your career, indicate the behavioral concept into which you were placed:

_____

_____

_____

_____

Regardless of the particular exercise that might be used in this part of the mentor training program, this activity is essential. The following assumptions are made relative to understanding and appreciating alternative styles:

1. People behave according to different behavioral styles. This situation occurs because people differ in how they perceive situations, work at tasks, interact with others, and make decisions.

2. People behave differently depending on the circumstances. In short, behavior changes.

3. There is no single "right" way for people to behave, but most people have an operating style that is most common and comfortable for them.

4. What feels comfortable and "right" to one person might feel uncomfortable and "wrong" to another.

5. An organization functions best when it capitalizes on the strengths of each individual and encourages the celebration of differences.

Appendix B includes a number of brief scenarios that show how an appreciation of different styles by protégés and mentors can be helpful in promoting more effective relationships.

Domain 4: Mentor Process Skills

In this part of training, the major skills that are needed to carry out actual mentoring relationships are identified and described. These are the three major skill areas that are typically addressed:

- Problem-solving skills
- Listening skills
- Observation skills

The essence of effective administration involves the resolution of problems that people in organizations face. As a result, mentoring relationships for administrators must be directed toward the discovery of ways to refine problem-solving skills.

The following seven steps can be used to assist administrative colleagues with analyzing and resolving problems that they face on the job. These steps can also be used to assist mentors in dealing with problems that they face as they work with protégés:

1. **Seek information about the problem in question.** If the existence of a particular problem is verified, this information can be useful for subsequent steps in this process.

2. **Define the problem.** Identify the desired situation and compare it to the actual one. Moving from the actual to the desired situation is the goal of problem solving.

3. **Propose alternative strategies.** To solve the problem, generate as many potential strategies as possible. Hold evaluations of the feasibility of these solutions until later in the process.

4. **Select the strategies that will actually be implemented.** After weighing the advantages and disadvantages of each proposed alternative strategy, choose the ones that are most likely to succeed.

5. **Design an implementation/action plan.** Translate your alternative strategies into specific actions; agree on who will be responsible for doing what tasks; identify and secure needed resources; set a timeline; and plan to assess the value of the actions that were actually taken.

6. **Implement the plan.**

7. **Assess the implementation/action plan.** Did the action plan produce the desired situation that was identified in the first step of this process? Continue, modify, or abandon the action plan depending on the outcome of the assessment.

You might wish to suggest to mentors that they review these seven basic steps so they are ready the first time the administrators with whom they are working encounter problems that might call for this type of linear problem-solving model. Another effective technique involves examining and reviewing these steps as administrative protégés are asked to work through the particular problems and issues that they face on the job.

With regard to conferencing skills, much of the interaction between mentors and protégés takes place during one-on-one situations. Some information in the general literature that is related to teacher supervision, particularly in the area of clinical supervision, might be helpful to mentors who are seeking appropriate ways to work with protégés. Administrative mentors need to adapt information that is presented in the literature in order to address the needs, concerns, and sensitivities that are found in administrative mentor-protégé conferences.

The purpose of conferencing between practicing administrators might be to address the following objectives:

- Promoting the sharing of experiences and gaining support from a colleague

- Promoting open communication

- Sharing problems, generating alternative solutions, and selecting appropriate and feasible alternatives

- Assisting mentors and protégés regarding particular problems

- Providing assistance and encouragement

- Providing for a support work environment so that both mentors and protégés can feel as if they are achieving professional growth and learning

In concrete terms, this part of the training strongly suggests that the conferencing between mentors and protégés should be based on periodic on-site visitations and observations of each other's work in school. After these visitations and observations take place, some of the questions that might be addressed by mentors and protégés include the following:

- What did you see when you watched the other administrator?

- What did you infer from his or her behavior?

- What insights did you gain into your own behavior after observing the behavior of the other administrator?

- How would you change your own behavior after what you have seen?

- In what ways do you believe that you are more effective as an instructional leader after the behavior that have observed?

What might be some additional questions to consider after you have had the opportunity to discuss your interaction and observations of an administrative colleague in your district?

_____

_____

_____

_____

_____

Finally, with regard to the process of identifying the observation skills that are needed by individuals who are serving as administrative mentors, the important point to emphasize is that observation in this context is considerably different from the kinds of skills that are used by administrators when observing teachers. After all, it is not possible to schedule a drop-in observation to see someone administer a school.

A recommended practice for those who wish to see what other administrators are doing is to engage in on-the-job shadowing. Here, one administrator agrees to follow a colleague around during a typical workday. During that period of shadowing, the observer says nothing and avoids any direct involvement in the activities of her or his partner. The emphasis is on complete, nonparticipant observation. The amount of time that is devoted to the shadowing will vary according to the time constraints of the partner administrators. It should be of sufficient duration that the observer can gain insights into a typical period of time in the life of the other administrator, however. The most important feature of the shadowing experience comes after the period of observation has concluded and when the two parties engage in the type of open, reflective conferencing that we described previously in this chapter.

What are some of the advantages that you see in promoting nonjudgmental shadow visits by administrators to other schools in your district?

_____

_____

Domain 5: Local Implementation Issues

Although the domains that are included in the training described here attempt to deal with as many issues as possible that will be encountered by mentors, it is also important to note that attention must be paid to the nature of local conditions and issues that exist in different states, schools, and districts. Time must be devoted to an examination of those local issues so that your mentoring program will fit into existing practices and programs. If it does not, it will likely be seen as just one more add-on responsibility to fill up the already crowded calendars of school administrators in the system.

The following topics are among the many that need to be considered at the local school district level as the district moves toward the implementation of a mentoring program for administrators:

- Is there a commitment by the central office and school board?
- Does mentoring fit with local board policy?
- Who will be involved with planning the program?
- How will individual needs be assessed?
- How will a budget be handled?
- What will our local program look like? What will be our structure?
- What are our goals and objectives?
- How will we know that our program goals and objectives have been met?

What additional questions do you believe you will need to consider in your own school system?

Checking Your Plan

In Chapter 2, some issues were presented that might be included in a comprehensive plan that is designed to help you establish a local mentoring program. Return to that outline and see how far you have progressed in the section dealing with mentor training.

A. Is orientation planned for the mentors?

_____ Yes _____ No

1. Are goals and objectives for mentor orientation listed?

_____ Yes _____ No

2. Is there a tentative schedule of activities for mentor orientation?

_____ Yes _____ No

3. Does the plan for mentor orientation include making mentors aware of the following:

a. Their roles and responsibilities

_____ Yes _____ No

b. Mentor training activities in which they will participate

_____ Yes _____ No

c. Support, rewards, and incentives for mentors

_____ Yes _____ No

d. Your district's procedures for evaluating mentor performance

_____ Yes _____ No

B. Is there a plan to have preliminary training for new mentors following the mentor orientation and prior to the initiation of mentoring?

_____ Yes _____ No

1. Are the goals and objectives for preliminary mentor training listed?

_____ Yes _____ No

2. Is there a schedule of activities for preliminary mentor training?

_____ Yes _____ No

3. Do goals, objectives, and activities in the preliminary mentor training plan focus on knowledge and skills that will be needed by mentors during the first few weeks of mentoring?

_____ Yes _____ No

C. Is there a plan for long-term mentor training?

_____ Yes _____ No

1. Are goals and objectives for long-term mentor training listed?

_____ Yes _____ No

2. Is there a schedule of activities for long-term mentor training?

_____ Yes _____ No

D. Are there plans for mentor orientation, preliminary training for new mentors, and long-term mentor training based on the development of a preliminary needs assessment?

_____ Yes _____ No

E. Are all elements of the plan for mentor training consistent with the following:

1. The purpose of the overall program of professional development in your district

_____ Yes _____ No

2. The rationale, goals, and objectives of your district's plan for administrative professional development

_____ Yes _____ No

F. Are human resources identified to coordinate and implement each planned mentor training activity?

_____ Yes _____ No

G. Are material resources identified that are necessary to carry out mentor training?

_____ Yes _____ No

Summarizing the Chapter

This chapter presented a plan for training individuals to serve as mentors to their administrative colleagues. We noted three purposes of the training:

- Participants need to be presented with the basic definition and understanding of mentoring as an effective approach to professional development.

- Individuals need to gain insights into personal behaviors that are related to effective administrative mentoring.

- People need to learn and practice the skills that are associated with effective mentoring for school administrators.

6

The Match Game

Assuming that you have worked very deliberately at setting up your mentoring program (as described in Part I) and that you have spent a lot of time selecting and training your mentors (as discussed in Chapters 4 and 5), what could possibly go wrong with your program? Unfortunately, the answer to that question is "plenty" if you ignore the material that is presented in this chapter.

This chapter considers how to match mentors with protégés. This topic might sound like a relatively simple matter, but it is more difficult than most people assume. Putting the wrong people together as mentors and protégés can be an extremely serious problem—one that could cause all of your hard work in establishing the program to be wasted. This situation is very similar to a couple who spends a lot of time together during a wonderful courtship, then spends many blissful hours arranging a beautiful wedding, and finally spends enthusiastic and happy days together on a romantic honeymoon —only to discover that the marriage will not last because the original match was not very good. There are many cases in which mentoring relationships have ended in bitter and unhappy "divorce" proceedings because the original courtship ignored some important signals.

A Case of a Bad Match

Sharee Daniels was a rookie elementary principal who had really thrown herself into this first administrative job. It was a dream come true for her to find this job after spending 16 years in the elementary classroom. She was widely recognized as an outstanding teacher in her district, but she grew uneasy in her role in the classroom. She wanted some new challenges.

Perhaps it was the fact that her husband was an administrator in the district, or perhaps it was because Sharee was a local kid who had gone to school in the district in which she had worked as a teacher. In any case, she was tired of being in her same district for so long, and she was now extremely happy to have found her own job—her own niche—as a real-life, honest-to-goodness principal in a new school system that was several miles away from her past life.

Now, she was on her own as a new principal. Despite this feeling of happiness at starting a new professional life, however, Sharee was also aware of the fact that as a rookie, she needed someone to help her with the many questions that seemed to come up every day on the job. Fortunately, her district had initiated a program a few years earlier to support beginning principals, and part of that program involved experienced administrators serving as mentors to newcomers. Because Sharee was a woman and an elementary school principal, it was an easy choice for the district to find a mentor. Rita Spencer, a nine-year veteran of the principalship, was the only other woman elementary principal in the district, so she was assigned to work with Sharee.

From the beginning, it was clear that conflicts were going to arise between Sharee and Rita. Sharee had an outgoing personality, whereas Rita was reserved and shy and generally preferred not to engage in any social conversation. On the other hand, Sharee was an optimist who wanted to see every experience as an opportunity to learn more about her new role.

Rita was typically negative and quite cynical. She was tired of being a principal, so she responded to most of Sharee's questions with one-word or two-word answers (usually followed by some criticism of the school district or other administrators).

What had started out to be an exciting year in Sharee's mind was now turning into a nightmare. She needed a mentor, but the one that she had been given was serving as anything but a positive role model, supporter, or confidante. In short, Sharee was only halfway through the first year of her life as a school leader, but she was already thinking about leaving the system.

How could the district have identified a better mentor for Sharee?

_____

_____

_____

_____

_____

_____

Mentor Matching: Some Myths

Many of the myths that are often associated with the matching of school administrators with effective mentors are highlighted in the case involving Sharee Daniels. For example, it is generally assumed that because Sharee was a woman, she needed a woman to serve as a mentor. Also, it is widely believed that mentors must come from the same level of schooling in which their protégés work; that is, only elementary administrators can serve as mentors to elementary administrators. Neither of these beliefs is supported in the research regarding the most appropriate ways of matching people in mentoring programs.

With regard to the first issue of matching genders for mentoring, studies of gender differences indicate that women prefer to have women as mentors, but there are no clear suggestions that women necessarily make better mentors to female colleagues. You should also remember that in many school systems, there are no women who are currently serving as school administrators. But it is critical to note that matching mentors with protégés should be based on more than gender. The same responses would be given in the case of providing mentor support to racial or ethnic minority representatives.

With regard to the second myth that mentoring must be only within the same level of schooling, by such reasoning secondary principals cannot possibly learn from elementary school principal mentors. Although it might be true that many technical parts of the administration of secondary schools differ from those of elementary schools, the foundations of school leadership, as defined by much of the literature dealing with effective leaders, remain the same in elementary, middle, senior high, or even postsecondary schools. Issues that are associated with the development of personal visions, for example, are the same in any type of organization. As a result, true mentoring can easily occur across different types of schools or even across school districts.

Another common belief regarding mentoring relationships is that mentors must be older than their protégés. Such a view is probably derived from common sense, and it is certainly consistent with one image of the mentor as the wise and more experienced colleague who knows all of the answers and who can provide the answers to the "new kids." As noted in Chapter 4, however, in the earlier description of the characteristics of effective mentors, the primary role of a mentor is not to know all of the answers but rather to work with a protégé to develop common understandings and solutions to concerns, issues, and problems that might occur in practice. A person's age has little bearing on one's ability to mentor. There are numerous examples of younger colleagues guiding and mentoring older colleagues. Furthermore, if this were not the case, it would not be possible to establish and support mentoring programs designed for all administrators in a district. Peer relationships in such settings are critical for success. There are simply no absolute and persistent findings to show that those mentors who are younger than their protégés are not able to serve as effective mentors.

Finally, there are many people who suggest that mentoring relationships must be built upon the geographical proximity of mentors and protégés. In other words, if mentors and protégés are not able to be together on a regular basis, mentoring relationships will be ineffective. Much of the logic underlying this view comes from the literature that describes successful mentoring programs for classroom teachers. The common view is that such programs depend on the likelihood that the partners in the mentoring relationship can drop in whenever they have a question to pose to their colleague. Under this assumption, particularly in more rural parts of the country, it would not be possible to develop mentoring programs in which administrators were always near enough to one another that frequent drop-in visits are possible. To the contrary, however, effective mentoring programs have been introduced into sparsely populated regions—and as a result, the criterion of geographical proximity does not need to become a powerful determinant of mentor-protégé matches.

So, What Criteria Should You Use?

The answer to this question is about as diverse as the number of school districts that are likely to adopt mentoring programs in the future. One district might have special conditions and characteristics that make it necessary to match mentors and protégés by using criteria that are quite different from those used in another school district. For example, in very rural areas, it might be impossible to develop a matching arrangement that is sensitive to many factors beyond those of geographical proximity of mentors and protégés. The same would be true where there might be only one administrator in a school district. If a mentoring program is started in such a situation, it would probably involve arranging for mentors and protégés to work across school district boundaries. In that case, the choice of mentoring selection criteria would be greatly reduced again.

In most cases, however, geography is not such that it makes the choice of effective strategies for matching mentors and protégés quite so problematic. As a result, the following are possible considerations of ways to bring pairs of administrators together for mutual support:

1. **Learning styles**—One way in which there can be some effective sharing between partners in mentoring teams is if they are brought together based on learning styles. Concrete and sequential learners might be better when working together, for example. One of the instruments that is often suggested for this purpose is the

Adult Learning Style Inventory developed by David Kolb. (Additional information concerning this resource is found in the Suggested Readings section at the end of this book.)

2. **Leadership styles**—Another excellent way of bringing protégés and mentors together is through a review of leadership styles, as measured by a wide array of instruments that are available and frequently used with administrators in school systems. It might not always be desirable to match people who have the same leadership style. In fact, rich mentor-protégé relationships often occur as the product of different leadership styles coming together. (Further information about possible resources in this area appears in the Suggested Readings section of this book.)

3. **Common philosophies/educational platforms**—The articulation of one's personal educational platform as a frequent activity is an excellent form of professional development. It is a way in which a person is able to indicate a variety of personal values and beliefs regarding significant educational issues. As noted in Chapter 5, part of the training for mentors should be devoted to the development of these personalized statements. These statements should be shared, and that sharing can serve as an excellent foundation for matching to occur between mentors and protégés.

What other issues and factors might serve as the basis for matching between the administrators who serve as mentors and protégés in your school district?

_____

_____

_____

_____

_____

_____

Some Additional Thoughts

Matching mentors with protégés in a structured, sensible, and sensitive fashion is neither easy nor precise. It would be highly desirable to match every school administrator with a mentor who possesses a sincere and deep desire to spend time working productively with a colleague. The fact is, however, that such commitments are not always available—particularly in very small school systems in which few administrators are available to serve as mentors or are qualified to serve according to the terms described in Chapter 4.

The ideal matching of mentors and protégés should always be based on an analysis of professional goals, interpersonal styles and values, and the learning needs of both parties. It is nearly impossible in the real world to engage in such perfect matching practices. Most mentoring relationships will likely be formed as marriages of convenience and not as ideal, naturally developing relationships that are so often presented in the literature on organizational practices. If individual awareness of (a) the values to be found in mentoring, (b) a regard for mutual respect and trust, and (c) a sense of openness and positive interaction are all present, however, then the mentor-protégé relationship has the potential to become very strong.

No magic recipes exist to guide the matching of mentors to protégés. Some of the issues that you might wish to consider in your school district, however, include the following:

1. **Cross-gender mentoring**—Despite the fact that research has not shown this issue to be either a positive or negative factor in the matching process, it is still an issue that must be considered at the local level. Will it be possible in your district for men to work effectively with female colleagues (or vice versa)? (Remember that there are often broader concerns raised in this regard. Mentors and protégés must often work after hours to discuss issues. Is this situation likely to cause concerns or problems because of the potential appearance of impropriety?)

2. **Mentoring across organizational levels**—Can the superintendent serve as a mentor to principals? Do you want to establish a program in which secondary school principals work with elementary administrators?

3. **Differences in ages**—Can younger but more experienced administrators serve as effective mentors to older colleagues who are just beginning their administrative careers? Can they serve as mentors to administrators who have experience and who are coming into your school system from another district? (This issue is now being faced in many private businesses in which a new generation of young leaders who are well versed in the technology of e-commerce is now working with senior executives who have many years of more traditional business experience but little knowledge of recent technological developments.)

4. **Mentoring across school systems**—Is it necessary for the mentor and protégé to be employed by the same school system? Can productive mentoring relationships be developed across school district boundaries?

At the local level, you must address the answers to these and other questions that are related to strategies that can be used to match mentors with protégés. Local conditions such as (a) the personalities of mentor administrators and other educational leaders, (b) traditions of cooperation, and (c) other aspects of life in particular school systems have a major impact on the way that your program might be developed.

Checking Your Plan

Now, return to the plan that you and your mentoring planning team developed, and use the outline in Chapter 2 of this book. Review your responses to each of the following questions that deal with the matching of mentors and protégés:

A. Are there criteria established for assigning mentors?

_____ Yes _____ No

1. Are the criteria compatible with the knowledge base on matching mentors and protégés?

_____ Yes _____ No

2. Do the criteria reflect practical considerations of the program size, types, and numbers of potential mentors?

_____ Yes _____ No

B. Is there a description of the procedures for matching mentors and protégés?

_____ Yes _____ No

1. Are the procedures compatible with the knowledge base related to mentor matching?

_____ Yes _____ No

2. Do the procedures address the concerns of those directly affected by mentor assignment?

_____ Yes _____ No

3. Is the issue of reassignment of mentors during the school year addressed?

_____ Yes _____ No

C. Are criteria and procedures for matching mentors and protégés compatible with the following:

1. The overall purposes of administrative professional development in your district

   _____ Yes   _____ No

2. The rationale, goals, and objectives of your district's professional development program

   _____ Yes   _____ No

Summarizing the Chapter

This chapter addressed a number of issues dealing with bringing mentors and protégés together in some reasonable fashion. There are no perfect answers to the questions about how to bring people together for effective professional development relations.

Despite limitations on absolute, correct answers for mentor-protégé matching, however, this issue has a lot to do with the overall perceptions of the program's effectiveness. A good system should offer the kind of flexibility in which it is possible for individual administrators to identify and work with multiple mentors throughout their careers. After all, in mentoring, long-term bonding between two people is not always a virtue. At times, it might be the most ineffective approach to a positive and mutually enhancing relationship.

7

Now That You Are a Mentor, What Do You Do?

THIS QUESTION HAS BEEN ASKED more than a few times as new mentoring programs have been launched in school districts across the nation. The lack of response to this question has been the greatest single cause of programs disappearing after they have been initiated.

People generally like the idea of starting a program of support for school administrators, whether the administrators are beginners or veterans. Mentoring is an appealing concept. Even when additional resources have to be found in order to initiate mentoring, this effort is not in itself a major inhibitor to the implementation and maintenance of a program.

The one obstacle that does serve to discourage people to the extent that they ultimately decide to give up on mentoring is feeling as if they do not know what they are supposed to do in their assigned jobs. Research on adult learning and development consistently shows that (a) adults do not wish to feel as if they are incompetent—that they cannot do something to which they have been assigned; (b) people feel frustrated because they cannot master some skill, such as using a particular computer program; and (c) people sometimes feel inadequate to serve effectively as mentors for colleague administrators (no one wants to fail at an important task).

A Case in Point

The Mountain Glen School District expected many new principals to assume leadership jobs in the next 3 to 5 years. When the district decided to adopt a new mentoring program in order to assist these new principals, there was considerable enthusiasm among the current administrators. Jack Gilhooly was particularly happy to volunteer as one of the five district administrators who would go through special training in mentor development so that he could be a resource to inexperienced colleagues in the future.

After all, he could remember quite vividly the frustration he felt about 10 years earlier when he first came on board as an assistant principal in the district. He knew so little, but everyone expected him to know everything (or so he believed). It was really a time in his professional life that he would just as soon forget.

Jack was most pleased to hear that the old sink-or-swim notion of bringing new administrators into the district was changing, and this mentoring program seemed to be a major commitment toward providing help. He attended the training sessions, developed a personal vision of what the value of mentoring would be, and now he was looking forward to working with Karen Saperstein, a new elementary principal in this district who had been assigned to Jack as a protégé. As directed during the mentor training session, Jack had taken the initiative to schedule the first two meetings with Karen, both of which were directed simply toward having each partner in the relationship learn more about the other. Karen struck him as a most agreeable individual who had a great deal of potential as a strong instructional leader for the district. It was quite apparent, too, that Karen had a considerable amount of apprehension about the next year. Like many beginning principals that Jack had seen in the past, Karen had clearly spent so much time finding this first job that she had not really figured out what she would be doing when she took control of her elementary school. She was excited but extremely anxious. Jack wanted to help as much as possible.

In coaching and mentoring Karen so that she can reach her greatest potential, what are some key issues that you feel Jack should share with Karen as she begins her new professional role?

Issue 1:

_____

Issue 2:

_____

Issue 3:

_____

There are a variety of essential skill areas in which a mentor can assist people when they assume a new administrative role or even help people with administrative experience perform their roles more effectively. Some of these include the following:

- **Framing issues**—For an individual who is taking on a new administrative position, the job can be overwhelming—considering all of the issues that need to be addressed. The first thing that you need to do when you begin working with a protégé is to frame the broad issues to be considered. For example, your protégé might discover that he or she has inherited several teachers who, to put it mildly, perform at only a marginal level. Although it is easy to identify and frame a problem such as this one, other issues might require a little more discussion.

It is critical that both the mentor and protégé (either a beginning administrator or veteran) establish some basic rules about openness and honesty in the discussion of all issues. Some issues might become the subjects of ongoing discussions (for instance, learning how to motivate classroom teachers). By contrast, other issues have a much shorter shelf life. An example of this situation might be setting up an effective parent-teacher conference schedule.

- **Identifying goals**—Once the mentor has worked with the protégé in order to identify some of the broad issues that need to be addressed, it is possible to look at long-term and immediate personal and professional goals. In a positive working relationship between a mentor and a protégé, it is helpful for a mentor to guide and support the aspirations of the protégé. Although the mentor can help the protégé focus on long-term goals, a more immediate goal should be to address a particular problem at each mentoring session.

Regardless of whether the mentoring is helping the protégé articulate long-term or immediate goals, you might find the following key ideas about goal setting valuable:

- Goals should be achievable and realistic.

- They should be measurable in terms of quality, quantity, or time.

- Ideally, they should be totally agreed upon by both the mentor and the protégé, but it is the protégé who should be responsible for initially proposing them.

- **Promoting self-directed learning**—A big part of the job of the mentor, particularly when working with new administrators, is to help the protégé grow into the new role. The key to a successful mentorship is the extent to which the protégé becomes comfortable with taking greater control of personal learning experiences. In short, the goal of good mentoring should be to make the protégé's reliance on the mentor eventually disappear.

There are a number of guidelines that you can follow in order to increase a protégé's self-directed learning:

- *Listen Actively*—Let protégés explain their concerns, fears, hopes, goals, or anything else that might be on their minds. Avoid the temptation to step in with, "It sounds to me that what you're trying to say is ..." Many mentors are tempted to intervene too quickly. It is important that the mentor begin the relationship by simply *listening* to the protégé.

- *Help Protégés Understand the Consequences of Their Actions*—The worst thing that a mentor can do is to tell protégés that they should not do something "because I know it won't work." Instead, the mentor should try to assist the protégé with understanding why something should (or should not) be done by asking, "What do you think might happen if you made that decision?"

- *Share Experiences*—Let protégés understand that even the worst mistakes have been made before. No one, not even the wisest and most experienced mentor, has had a perfect track record as an administrator. "We all make mistakes" might be a very powerful observation to share.

- **Establishing limits**—Protégés might become frustrated if they discover that mentors have not been completely open about the limitations of certain courses of action before they were taken. Although it might be desirable to encourage protégés to take risks and be creative, mentors should clearly state any restrictions that might apply to a particular approach.

  The job of the mentor is to try to find the appropriate balance between supporting innovative and creative approaches to administration on the part of protégés and remaining honest and candid about limitations.

- **Empowering for action**—Mentoring is a means of assisting and guiding the work of others. Mentors become increasingly effective as protégés decrease their reliance, however.

  This situation is achieved through the mentor's willingness to empower protégés. A mentor can do three things to build a sense of empowerment in protégés:

  - Encourage protégés to do most of the talking while making use of nondirective consultative skills.

  - Encourage protégés to move from the role of a student to the role of a teacher and become the leaders of mentor-protégé relationships (protégés are not the only learners in the relationship).

  - Remain open and honest with their protégés (they must be prepared to give the straight scoop).

  Empowering for action also implies that the mentor serves as a mediator within an organization. There are times when an experienced administrator in a district knows the right way to get things done (who to call, what forms to fill out, who to listen to, who to ignore, and so forth).

- **Summarizing**—An effective mentor must, in discussion with the protégé, summarize any agreements that are reached. This procedure ensures a complete understanding of what has been discussed and what plans have been made.

It is far better for mentors to check for shared understanding while there is direct contact between themselves and protégés than to try to fix the results of missed communication later.

Additional Responsibilities of Mentors

In very general terms, mentors are able to work with individual protégés to help build the following:

- Feelings of personal and professional competence
- Self-confidence
- A greater sense of self-direction
- Increased professionalism

Mentors can also provide assistance to other administrators in at least five additional areas that are traditionally associated with effective performance of instructional leaders:

1. Gaining knowledge of the district's curriculum and available instructional resources

2. Sharing information about leadership practices that are effective in helping teachers improve their instructional skills and classroom-management skills

3. Serving as role models for completing managerial tasks

4. Sharing effective strategies and practices for developing positive school-community relations

5. Helping protégés formulate personalized insights into developing productive, satisfying work environments for teachers so that student learning outcomes can be improved

What are some of the other responsibilities that can be identified for mentors in your school district as they help colleagues grow as instructional leaders?

_____

_____

_____

_____

_____

_____

Consultation Skills

Mentor-protégé relationships are based on a number of fundamental skills that are used in consultation settings. The following are skills that effective mentors need to exhibit:

- Listening to others

- Sharing information

- Treating others with respect

- Facilitating team membership

- Using situational leadership

- Developing informal relationships

- Giving feedback and being open to receiving feedback

- Giving others credit for their ideas

- Demonstrating a willingness to learn from others

- Recognizing and responding to individual differences

Return to the case study found at the beginning of this chapter and assume that you are Karen's mentor. What if Karen came to you with a problem concerning her relationship with her building custodian who was not completing tasks assigned to him within a designated timeline? Karen indicates to you that her goal is to provide a clean and safe environment for students and staff. She wants certain tasks in the building to be completed, but she is not sure of the custodian's job description, and she does not know how to approach him in a professional manner that will let him know that she is unhappy about his performance. It is early August, and Karen is eager to ensure that her building will be ready for teachers, but she does not want to start the school year on the wrong foot by establishing a negative relationship with her custodian. How would you use the 10 steps listed previously to work through this issue with Karen?

Listen to others

_____

_____

Share information

_____

_____

Treat others with respect

_____

_____

Facilitate team membership

_____

_____

Use situational leadership

_____

_____

Develop informal relationships

_____

_____

Give feedback and be open to feedback

_____

_____

Give others credit for their ideas

_____

_____

Demonstrate a willingness to learn from others

_____

_____

Recognize and respond to individual differences

_____

_____

Developing an Action Plan

An important part of forming an effective mentor-protégé relationship is to make certain that there is a high degree of clarity regarding the interactions that are expected to occur over time. As a result, a practical suggestion is that mentors and protégés should work out a clear action plan early in the school year. This action plan would involve the identification of priority goals, specific objectives, activities that assist the protégé with reaching the stated goals and objectives, and some way of identifying whether or not the goals and objectives have been achieved. Appendix C includes a mentor-protégé action planning form that might be helpful to you when carrying out this type of mentor-protégé action planning.

Checking Your Plan

Review your plan for mentor job descriptions as developed in this chapter and compare it to the plan that you have established for implementation.

  A. Are program responsibilities of your school district's central office, responsibilities at the building level, and responsibilities of other organizations involved in the mentoring program clearly defined and delineated?

   _____ Yes _____ No

  B. Are the roles and responsibilities of all people involved in the mentoring program clearly defined?

   _____ Yes _____ No

  C. Supports and rewards

   1. Are provisions made for regular group meetings that focus on support for mentors?

    _____ Yes _____ No

   2. Is a support person identified to coordinate the activities of mentors?

    _____ Yes _____ No

3. Are mentors provided with sufficient time to carry out their responsibilities?

_____ Yes _____ No

4. Are provisions made for mentors to receive resources essential for carrying out their mentoring responsibilities?

_____ Yes _____ No

D. Rewards and mentors

1. Are there extrinsic rewards for mentors such as financial rewards or additional release time?

_____ Yes _____ No

2. Are there provisions for school district recognition of particularly effective mentors?

_____ Yes _____ No

3. Are there incentives for mentors to engage in individualized activities to promote their personal and professional development?

_____ Yes _____ No

E. Are all elements of the plan for providing support and rewards for mentors compatible with the following:

1. The purposes of your district's professional development program

_____ Yes _____ No

2. The rationale, goals, and objectives of your district's professional development program

_____ Yes _____ No

F. Are human resources identified to coordinate support and rewards for mentors?

_____ Yes _____ No

G. Are material resources identified that are necessary to provide support and rewards for mentors?

_____ Yes _____ No

Summarizing the Chapter

In this chapter, a number of ideas were presented to help you answer the important question, "So, now that I am a mentor, what do I do?" Mentor-protégé relationships are viewed as most effective (a) when they are developed so that they demonstrate warmth and respect between the parties, and (b) when they serve as motivators for the mentor and protégé to grow professionally. Effective mentoring requires a commitment of time, energy, and effort. But all of this hard work pays off in terms of extremely positive outcomes for mentors, protégés, and school districts.

There are no magic answers to questions about specific mentoring activities. The simplest suggestions are critical to successful relationship building, however. As a result, you might wish to consider the following suggestions as key ideas to include as you work with colleagues as protégés in the process:

- Smile and be pleasant.

- Praise and celebrate your colleague's successes.

- Encourage your colleague to be the best that he or she can be.

- Focus on strengths, not weaknesses.

- Display confidence in the ability and judgment of your colleague.

- Support the mentoring relationship.

- Help your colleague realize and build upon present skills and abilities.

8

Mentoring for Beginning Leaders

ONE OF THE AREAS in which school districts have focused increasing attention related to professional development for school leaders is the area of support for those who are at the beginning stages of their careers. A strategy that is an effective tool for this type of induction program is the use of mentors or experienced administrators who are recruited to "show the ropes" to the new folks.

As indicated throughout the earlier chapters of this book, effective mentoring must be understood as a process that is much more sophisticated than simply sharing craft knowledge when called upon by organizational newcomers. It must be seen as a proactive instructional process in which a learning contract is established between the mentor and the protégé. Like any other form of effective teaching, mentoring must include an investment of time and commitment on the part of both the teacher and the learner. Furthermore, effective mentoring must involve a sharing of information that goes beyond answering questions that come up when people are trying to survive on the job. Mentoring involves the creation and maintenance of a mutually enhancing relationship in which both the mentor and the protégé can attain goals that are related to both personal development and career enhancement.

Mentoring can be a particularly effective process to help the beginning school leader. To emphasize this fact, consider what it was like when you first became a school administrator (or teacher, or counselor, or virtually any other position in any type of organization). What are some of the questions and issues that you considered during your first year?

1. _____

2. _____

3. _____

4. _____

5. _____

Now, list some of the ways in which a person who might have served in the role of an assigned mentor could have assisted you in dealing with any of these issues.

1. Issue:

_____

_____

My mentor could have helped me by:

_____

_____

_____

2. Issue:

_____

_____

My mentor could have helped me by:

_____

_____

_____

3. Issue:

_____

_____

My mentor could have helped me by:

_____

_____

_____

4. Issue:

_____

_____

My mentor could have helped me by:

_____

_____

_____

5. Issue:

_____

_____

My mentor could have helped me by:

_____

_____

_____

Beginning Administrators' Needs

During the last few years, more and more research has been carried out in order to determine the kinds of problems encountered by beginning school administrators. These studies have shown that people who are in their first year of service in a school system tend to encounter problems in three distinct areas:

1. **Role clarification**—Understanding who they are, now that they are principals, and how they are to make use of their newly discovered authority

2. **Limitations on technical expertise**—How to do the things that they are supposed to do (according to job descriptions)

3. **Difficulties with socialization to the profession and individual school systems** —Learning how to do things in a particular setting (learning the ropes)

Beginning Principals: Two Cases

Anne Marie was in the middle of her first year as a new elementary principal of one of those school buildings that seemed to have been built in distinct stages over a period of about 75 years. The old wings were built shortly after World War I, and the new wings were built in the mid-1950s. In general, it was a fairly pleasant building, but she was discovering some problems.

In one corridor connecting an old wing to a newer part of the building, there were five steps—each of which was covered with tile that matched the material used on the rest of the floors and walls. One of the first things that Anne Marie noticed when she walked through her building in August was that a few of the step tiles were loose. She was concerned that as the year progressed, this situation could lead to a more serious problem and someone could be injured.

She consulted her district policy manual to determine the proper course of action. After several phone calls to the maintenance division, she learned that replacing the old tiles would require enough major repair work that she would need the approval of Dave Spencer, the maintenance division director. It was late August when she began the process of dutifully following all specified procedures and filling out the necessary forms to get the tile-covered steps replaced. It was now early November; the tiles were still loose; one child had already taken a tumble (fortunately without breaking any bones or threats of lawsuits from angry parents); and Anne Marie could not get the issue resolved with Dave.

Because she was a rookie, and because she did not want to rock the boat by not following procedures, she said nothing about her tale of the tile. Watching second and third graders slip on the floor week after week had frustrated her to the point where she decided to do something besides following channels, however. At last week's district elementary principals meeting, she shared her frustrations with Lionel Overturn, a veteran principal. She said that she was going to hire a contractor out of her own pocket if the repairs were not completed soon.

Lionel calmly indicated that veteran principals knew never to bother the maintenance director with requests about building repairs. "Everyone" knew that Dave had been placed in that position a few years ago because he had not been successful in some more visible managerial assignment, and he now had fewer than two years to go until retirement. Besides that, Lionel pointed out, "Everybody knows that Ralph Sanchez, the assistant superintendent for instruction, is the person to see about getting repairs done in your building. He was director of maintenance until Dave got the job. He sure knows how to make things happen."

Consider a second case. Tom Pistola was also nearing the end of the first half of his rookie year as an elementary principal in Cloverdale. He had moved to this system from another part of the state where he had spent the past 12 years as an elementary teacher.

He generally enjoyed his work to this point. One issue was frustrating him, however. When Tom started his job back in June, he naturally attended the school board meeting at which his contract was approved. In this school district, the board meets twice each month. Tom then attended every board meeting (a practice of principals that he had observed back in his old district) until he realized that he was typically the only building administrator in attendance. As a result, he decided not to attend another meeting, beginning with the second August session.

At the Wednesday principals meeting that followed the second August board meeting, Tom was greeted by three other principals who wanted to know why they had not seen him on Monday night at the school board meeting. Based on that signal, Tom again began to attend board meetings but again found himself the only principal there. On a few nights, however, every building administrator in the district came to the meeting—typically saying nothing.

Tom simply could not understand what was going on. He had other things to do on Monday nights. But he wanted to fit in as a new administrator in Cloverdale. He could not understand the signal that triggered attendance by principals at some meetings but not at others.

One day, Tom shared his concerns with Elizabeth Thatcher, a junior high school principal who had worked in the district for nearly 20 years. She admitted that although it was not a foolproof system, most principals had come to recognize when issues on the board agenda were ones that the central office wanted to gain support for by having a show of solidarity by building principals. The principals attended those meetings. Elizabeth volunteered to sit down with Tom a few days before every board meeting (after agendas were distributed to administrators) to decide whether or not the agenda contained any items that needed a show of solidarity.

How Could Mentoring Help?

1. Were these examples of problems with role clarification, limitations on technical expertise, difficulties with socialization, or some combination of these different issues?

   (Anne Marie's case):

   _____

   _____

   _____

   (Tom's case):

   _____

   _____

   _____

2. Were the two experienced principals (Lionel and Elizabeth) functioning as mentors in the ways that we have described in this book, or were they taking on some other helping roles?

   _____

   _____

   _____

   _____

3. How might a structured mentoring program be developed as a way to help the next generations of Anne Maries and Toms who are coming on board as principals for the first time?

   _____

   _____

   _____

   _____

In the cases of both Anne Marie and Tom, the major issues that they faced as beginning principals concerned socialization. Neither individual was able to read the subtle signs and practices that existed in their school systems. Anne Marie could hardly be expected to know in advance that the way to get the step tiles fixed was to skip over the maintenance division and go to the assistant superintendent for instruction. Also, Tom might have spent another six months trying to discern the pattern of agenda items that normally brought principals to the board meetings on Monday nights.

Although the behaviors of the experienced principals—Lionel and Elizabeth—were extremely helpful to their rookie colleagues, their interventions might not necessarily be classified as mentoring. For one thing, they helped only when the newcomers approached them. Second, the approach that both individuals used was to indicate that all of the experienced principals in the school districts would have known when to come to school board meetings or how to get the steps fixed. In short, they served as gatekeepers to inside information, not as guides and supporters who worked with the new principals on an ongoing basis.

Becoming a principal for the first time will naturally expose you to a large number of new situations for which you have no answers. No matter how well a person might have been prepared through a pre-service preparation program, taking a new job will always involve ambiguity and uncertainty. No one can see to it that a newcomer has no problems or questions along the way. But a structured mentoring program can be an important way to ensure that rookie principals (or superintendents or any others in leadership roles) are not simply left to wander through their first years without any ongoing direction. A good mentoring program will do more than create a paper network in which experienced administrators are assigned to answer questions from beginners on an as-needed basis. If your district adopts a structured mentoring program for beginning leaders, a definite plan should be established in order to guide the interactions that should take place on a regular basis between mentors and protégés. It is assumed that those who will serve as mentors have been selected on the basis of criteria noted in Chapter 4 and that a matching process similar to the one identified in Chapter 6 would have been followed.

Soon after a new principal is selected for a position in the district (but prior to the actual beginning of the school year), mentors might discuss some of the following technical skills and socialization topics with their protégés:

1. **Develop teacher/student/parent handbooks**—What is the purpose of these resource materials? How do they fit in with the district's goals? What are the deadlines that need to be addressed in their development?

2. **Inventory supplies**—Are the supplies needed to begin the school year in storage in the building? How do teachers have access to these materials? Where does one go to get additional materials?

3. **Check equipment**—Is everything in place for the start of the next school year? Was everything that was ordered last year actually delivered? Who does one talk to about problems?

4. **Inventory instructional materials**—Is everything ready? Where does one go if there are problems?

5. **Check teachers' duty schedules**—Does everyone know what they are supposed to do on the first day of school? If not, how does one fix the problem? What about new teachers?

6. **Determine whether it is necessary to do any last-minute hiring of teachers or other staff.**

7. **Establish schedules for "special" teachers**—Has this procedure already been done? What is the best way to go about doing this task?

List some of the same types of topics and issues that would need to be covered prior to the beginning of a school year by the principals in your district:

_____

_____

_____

_____

_____

_____

Besides these issues, mentors can be extremely helpful to beginning school principals by reviewing the following items that might be critical in dealing with many of the role clarification problems that novices often face:

- **Personal educational philosophy or platform of the beginning principal**—What are some of the most important and central educational values of the new person? What are the non-negotiable values that the new person believes should not be violated by the demands of the new job?

- **Vision**—What does the new administrator hope to accomplish during this first year on the job? Besides simply surviving and getting a new contract, what will be some of the indicators that the newcomer will look for as an affirmation of success this first year?

- **Personal identity**—What will it feel like to have teachers, parents, students, and others look to you as the authority figure who has all of the answers?

What are some other items of this nature that you believe should be covered before the school year begins?

_____

_____

_____

_____

_____

_____

In the first few weeks after the school year has begun, the following topics might ordinarily deserve some conversation between mentors and beginning administrators:

- How to oversee building operations, including the daily performance of custodial and clerical staff

- How to resolve difficulties associated with food service

- How to provide a safe and secure learning environment for students, teachers, and staff

- Housekeeping details (do not miss certain deadlines for important reports due to the state department of education, central office, and so forth)

Additional items to consider in your school district might include the following:

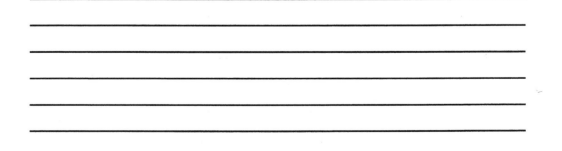

As the first school year progresses, the following technical topics might also be considered as part of the ongoing orientation discussions between the new administrator and his or her mentor:

- How to implement personnel policies, such as the use of professional leave days, sick days, and so forth

- Reminders of deadlines for the implementation of notifications of nonrenewals for teachers and for the district's mandated evaluation cycle

Other items that might be addressed throughout the school year in your district include the following:

_____

_____

_____

_____

_____

_____

The items listed here tend to be associated with helping people become oriented to a new school or district, and they are important. Simply going over these matters is not all there is to a mentoring program, however. As noted previously in the discussions of what might occur prior to the beginning of a school year, mentors and new administrators must have the opportunity to meet concerning socialization issues. These are things that will help a person who is in a position of visible authority feel more comfortable for the first time. Research also consistently shows that one area in which beginning administrators have the most difficulty is how to develop a clear understanding of themselves in a totally new role.

When it comes to socialization, it is more difficult to assign specific issues that need to be addressed at different times during a school year. Instead, discussions along these lines are best handled on an ongoing basis and as new administrators come forward with concerns. Some of the issues that might be covered, however, during face-to-face discussions include the following:

- Individual educational platforms and philosophies of education

- Ways in which the staff seems to be adjusting to the presence of a new administrator

- Strains in personal and family relationships that might be apparent as a result of the new job and its time demands

- Considerations of the subtle signs of evaluation in a district (how does the new person pick up signals that he or she is in trouble with the central office, for example)

- How you can tell whether you are doing a good job

Other issues that might be considered relative to how well a new administrator is fitting in are as follows:

_____

_____

_____

_____

_____

_____

Finally, mentors can assist newly hired administrators in other ways. Regardless of the competence and ability of people who were recently hired, it is likely that they will not possess all of the knowledge and skills that are expected of experienced administrators. As a result, discussions between new administrators and mentors might include the following:

- The prevailing computer knowledge expectations for all administrators and how to learn more if these skills are a problem

- The vision of effective teaching and learning and instruction that has been adopted by the system

Other similar issues that might warrant conversations between mentors and new administrators in your district are as follows:

_____

_____

_____

_____

_____

_____

Summarizing the Chapter

The information in this chapter was designed to help you with a mentoring program that is used to assist beginning school leaders in your school district. It might be possible that your system does not hire many rookies in any given year. If that is the case, you might wish to explore the possibility of working with other nearby districts to develop a program to assist all new administrators in a particular region. Some issues that are discussed between mentors and newcomers are district-specific. Many things that a new principal needs to know concern issues of a broader nature, however.

No matter what the local approach to a mentoring program for new administrators might look like, this chapter concludes by reminding you of a few important observations about people who are stepping into their first formal leadership roles:

- They need assistance and support in terms of learning how to (a) clarify their new role, (b) demonstrate technical skills related to their jobs, and (c) fit into a new social and professional setting.

- They will probably be apprehensive about seeking help from others. After all, the image of the administrator as a loner has been around for a long time.

- They will always want to get a colleague to tell them how they are doing on the job. They need this feedback frequently and honestly.

9

Mentoring for Veterans

CHAPTER 8 discussed the importance of developing mentoring programs that are geared toward helping beginning school administrators achieve initial success on the job. Such efforts are extremely important in promoting ongoing professional development for school administrators. Mentoring is a practice that can also be geared toward the needs of *all* administrators, however (regardless of experience).

This chapter presents some ideas that you can use to develop a mentoring program that will assist veteran administrators. As you will recall from Chapter 3, a primary (or even sole) focus of your work might be on this important group of professionals. The material presented here will be helpful to you as you look for a way to meet their learning needs.

Mentoring for Veterans: Two Cases

Frank Auschlander had been an elementary school principal in the Rolling Hills School District for 5 years. This school district was a very nice place that had good teachers and colleague administrators. But there had been a long history of community unrest in the Rolling Hills Schools over financial issues. As a result, Frank had been looking for a position in another school system for a year, and he was extremely happy when he was offered a position as a building principal at Jefferson Elementary School in the Richlands Estates Schools. All of the curriculum reforms that he wanted to promote in the past would now be possible. It would also be nice to go to work without always starting the day with a new rumor about how the local concerned citizens committee was going to get one teacher or another fired for doing something that was contrary to the committee's wishes.

From his first day on the new job at Richlands, it was clear to Frank that life was going to be considerably different from what it had been in Rolling Hills. Teachers seemed to be much more sophisticated; he did not have anyone in his building who had less than a master's degree and at least 10 years of experience. Rolling Hills seemed to have a revolving door, with teachers stopping in for only a year or two at a time so that they could get enough teaching experience to find a job in a better district.

At Richlands, community members were in Frank's building frequently, but they rarely presented him with grievances or petitions. At about the moment when Frank really thought he had died and gone to heaven by getting the new job in Richlands, he was startled one day when he was summoned to the office of the assistant superintendent for administrative services. He was asked to explain why he had offended a group of parents in his school by not supporting the local merchants' association's "Onward to Excellence" fair at the Richlands Shopping Center. Frank was surprised to hear of the complaint, given the fact that he believed all contact with the community to date had been quite positive. He told the assistant superintendent that he would talk to the concerned parents and try to do a better job of communicating in the future.

At the next district principals meeting, Frank shared this story with Gretchen Bailey, another experienced elementary principal who had arrived in Richlands only 2 years earlier. Gretchen smiled at Frank and said, "You'll learn the same way I did. These parents here appear very supportive, but there are more coffee klatch meetings here per block than anywhere else in the state. Don't be surprised if you keep getting attacked for one thing or another. It goes with the turf here in Richlands. This is a good school system, but you always have to be aware." Frank left the meeting wondering who would help keep him aware.

In what ways could a mentoring program for veteran administrators have helped Frank in his transition from Rolling Hills to Richlands?

Describe the ways in which administrators who have experience who come to your school district are provided with information and support as they start their jobs in your system:

_____

_____

_____

_____

_____

If this list is blank or if you must admit that your district does nothing to help veterans who come on board, do not be surprised. Very few school districts across the nation do anything to help with the transition problems faced by experienced leaders who are coming into a new setting. The prevailing model is one that suggests that if you have done it somewhere else, you know all of the answers. "That's why we hired you—so you wouldn't have to bother anyone" is a typical statement. This image is wrong and denies the fact that people often find ways to learn about new cultures, norms, practices, and expectations as they proceed from one school system to another in their careers. After all, it is not a case of "a school system is a school system is a school system . . . "

Consider another case. Mary Shelby has been the principal of Big Meadow High School, a large school that has nearly 2,000 students, for nearly 10 years. She started at Big Meadow as a teacher, then became an assistant principal, and is now the principal. She has spent her entire 22-year professional career in Big Meadow. In short, she knows the school, the district, the community, and the people around her.

Although Mary certainly knows much about her school and its environment, the one thing she really does not know much about are her colleague administrators in the district. She sees most of them at least once each month at district administrative team meetings, and some—her assistant principals Tom Finnegan, Makie Legothlo, and Nick Ramirez—she sees every day. In addition, Mary has had the opportunity to interact socially with most of the other principals and central office administrators. But seeing and knowing people in these settings still has not allowed Mary to really understand most of her colleagues professionally. What is even more frustrating to Mary is her belief that none of her coworkers really know much about her or appreciate her work, goals, or professional dreams. For years, she has known that the principalship is a lonely job, but she now feels as if she is becoming alienated from any real contact with her peers.

How could a mentoring program provide support for Mary and help her feel less isolated?

_____

_____

_____

_____

_____

_____

_____

How could a mentoring program in your district help serve the needs of experienced administrators?

_____

_____

_____

_____

_____

_____

Mentoring for Experienced Transfers

Throughout this book, we have presented a vision of mentoring for both beginning and veteran school administrators. Clearly, a different vision is needed for experienced transfers: newly hired administrators who have had experience in other school systems. You might assume that the issues that are associated with initial socialization to the profession of educational administration would have been addressed during the earlier phases of a person's career. A person who has been a principal in one school district will likely know how it feels to be the boss. But unlike beginning administrators, transfers are probably not going to experience many problems with role identity and perhaps only limited problems with the technical demands of the job.

On the other hand, many areas that are covered in a mentoring program for rookies can also be addressed to transfer administrators, particularly such things as initial orientation to a new school system and remediation of specific skills that are needed for performance in a new district. No matter how long a person might have served as an administrator in another school district, he or she has probably never worked in their new system. For example, even if a person has had extensive experience with the use of certain data-processing practices in some other setting, those practices might not be compatible with what is done in the new system. As a result, someone who is showing the newcomer "how we do it around here" can be quite helpful.

It might be necessary to provide needed information to an experienced administrator in the following areas:

1. What they are expected to know about computers and how to learn more if there is a problem

2. Orientation to the vision of effective teaching and learning that has been adopted by the system

What are some of the specific areas in which mentors might be able to assist experienced administrators who are newcomers to your district?

_____

_____

_____

_____

_____

_____

Mentoring for Veterans Within a System

Mentoring programs for beginning administrators are based on the assumption that those who are new to a school or to some other organization do not have all of the experience, knowledge, or basic skills that they need to do their jobs at the same level as others who are in the same system. This assumption is not valid for mentoring programs for practicing administrators who have been on the job for several years, particularly if those years have been in the same system. As opposed to the programs for rookies or even transfers, which address issues associated with a need for initial professional socialization or orientation, mentoring for veteran administrators is cast in an entirely different light. This last model of mentoring must be seen as a peer coaching strategy that would encourage pairs of administrators to work together in order to promote more effective, ongoing professional development. One program that has a lot to offer is *Peer-Assisted Leadership* (PAL), a program for administrator in-service that was developed by the Far West Regional Educational Laboratory in San Francisco, California. PAL is a simple concept. It suggests that experienced administrators can improve their own performance by observing and talking with other experienced administrators on an ongoing basis. There are two critical dimensions associated with this peer coaching model: shadowing and reflective interviewing.

Shadowing. Shadowing is a way for one administrator to observe a colleague's day-to-day activities—not as a form of evaluation or appraisal, but as a form of simple observation of what the other person is doing. Shadowing is meant to be a behavioral record of what observers see and hear as they follow the actions of professional partners.

The following are some important guidelines to be used in establishing this non-evaluative observation and shadowing program:

1. Partners should find a time period of two to four hours when it will be possible to visit each other's school during regular work hours.

2. Observations (shadows) should be as unobtrusive as possible. The person who is doing the observing should not interrupt activities or ask questions during the time of the shadowing.

3. The observer should follow the person who is being shadowed everywhere unless there is some indication that this action would not be appropriate.

4. Nonverbal communication during the shadowing experience should be avoided.

5. Prior arrangements should be made for handling sensitive situations.

6. After the end of the first shadowing experience, the participants should discuss the process to determine whether any adjustments should be made for the next time.

In what ways do you anticipate being able to make use of this shadowing technique in your local school system?

_____

_____

_____

_____

_____

_____

Reflective interviewing. Information that is obtained during the shadowing program is presented to the person who is being shadowed (mentored) during reflective interviews. The goal of the reflective interview is to clarify and understand the other administrator's observed actions by exploring meanings and consequences. The interviewer's responsibility is to assist and support his or her colleague in exploring observed activities, not to judge or evaluate him or her. The interviewer must create a safe environment in which differences are respected and information is treated confidentially.

The following procedures need to be followed in reflective interviewing:

1. Review field notes that are made during the shadowing process; highlight and identify specifically those items that need to be clarified during the interview.

2. Bring field notes and specific questions to the interview. The day's events during the shadowing process should be reconstructed with the person who was shadowed.

3. Record the responses to each question of the reflective interview. Accuracy should be checked with the person who is being interviewed.

4. Integrate the reflective interview notes with field notes so that the shadowing and interview notes will constitute one complete record.

In what ways do you anticipate being able to make use of reflective interviewing techniques when guiding the professional development of veteran school administrators in your district?

_____

_____

_____

_____

_____

_____

Checking Your Plan

The last two chapters looked at how you might develop administrator mentoring programs that are targeted at the specific needs of two different groups of school administrators: beginners and veterans. In Chapter 2, we suggested that an important part of your planning process would involve deciding the exact nature of the target group to be served by your mentoring program. Review the following list of planning items to see how your planning has gone so far:

A. Will your mentoring program be directed exclusively at the needs of beginning school administrators in your district, or will it be available to all administrators?

_____ Yes _____ No

B. Is there a clear understanding of the kinds of issues that need to be included in mentoring programs for beginning administrators (in contrast with topics that are more appropriate for veterans)?

_____ Yes _____ No

Summarizing the Chapter

This chapter provided information concerning the possible applications of a mentoring program that focuses on the learning and developmental needs of experienced school administrators in your district. There are two groups of experienced administrators: a) those who are new to your system but who have had experience in other districts, and b) those who are experienced administrators in your system.

Some of the important issues to be remembered when working with veteran administrators in a mentoring program are the following:

- The mentoring program cannot be perceived as evaluative in nature.

- Mentoring should be arranged in order to maximize peer coaching strategies rather than organized as implied hierarchical arrangements in which the mentor instructs the protégé.

- The program will be more difficult to sell because many experienced administrators have been socialized to the belief that they must never admit concerns to colleagues.

- Despite the previous statement, mentoring for veterans is important because most school administrators, when questioned individually, admit that they feel lonely and isolated in their roles. Mentoring is a way to reduce those feelings.

PART III

Assessing Your Program

IN GENERAL, this past year has been a good one for Harlan Green. He arrived as the superintendent last July and found the teachers, administrators, community, and school board extremely supportive. For the most part, they approved the things that he wanted to do. One thing that concerned him, however, was the new negative focus on administrative professional development that he had introduced into the district. He firmly believed that if leaders were not learners, the rest of the school system would ultimately suffer. Despite this personal conviction, there had been criticism that spending money and time in this area was somehow taking away resources that were directly available for children. In particular, there had been concern about the value of the new mentoring program that Harlan had initiated for the administrators throughout the district.

Arnie Fromeyer, a board member who had traditionally been very supportive of Harlan's programs, became the most vocal critic of the mentoring program. Last week, in an executive session of the school board, Arnie confronted Harlan by saying, "I can't really buy this stuff about the principals spending time going out to each other's buildings and talking about their problems all the time. We hired them—and you—to provide some leadership around here, not just to cry on each other's shoulders all day. Unless you can start to show that your new mentoring program is giving us some results, I'm afraid I'm going to push for an end to this kind of activity next year." Harlan now had to provide some proof that the training, planning, and all of the other mentoring activities are somehow worth it to a school board that has been generally supportive of the rest of the programs in the district.

This scenario is by no means an unrealistic one, and designers of local mentoring programs for school administrators need to be prepared to provide information to their own school boards and others who want to know whether programs have really shown any results. As noted in the first part of this book, mentoring programs do not necessarily cost a lot of money to develop and operate, but they do require resources. Perhaps what is more important is that they require some changes in the visible behaviors and action patterns of school administrators. Suddenly, superintendents, principals, and others are not independent experts who have all of the answers. Instead, they are members of a larger leadership team for the school district. That change is ultimately a good one. But it also means that people might perceive that principals are now wasting time by crying on each other's shoulders. That is a very unfortunate perception and definition of peer support and mentoring, but it is one that might be present in your community as well.

The most effective way to deal with criticism is with data and solid information that address concerns about overall program effectiveness and success. The last part of this book provides information that might be helpful to you when developing a program evaluation and assessment process. This step should be done before you actually implement your program. Chapter 11 ("What's Next?") also includes some of the ways in which you might follow up your mentoring program with additional professional development activities for your school district leadership team.

10

How Do We Know Whether It Worked?

THE QUESTION that serves as the title of this chapter is a very logical one and is an expected one for program planners and implementers. After all, planning for and implementing a mentoring program for school administrators—whether for only the beginners or for all of the administrators in your district—implies that a considerable amount of time, effort, and some financial resources will have to be invested in a new activity. It is reasonable to expect to see some degree of accountability as part of the program. Part of your initial planning for the adoption of mentoring should involve serious thoughts about how you will know whether what you planned to do has been achieved.

This chapter offers some suggestions for developing a framework that will enable you to determine whether all of your hard work has been worth it.

Case Study: A Remarkable Coincidence

The statewide administrators association has its annual conference in a beautiful mountain resort community each August. The association is an umbrella organization that includes superintendents, business officials, and elementary and secondary school principals from across the state. Many school board members also typically attend the meeting.

As is true in many other states, it has been recognized that there will be a need for many new administrators to come on board in the next few years. Early retirements and growth in several big districts in the state are causing many vacancies. Furthermore, there is recognition that the role of the school administrator is becoming increasingly complex and that new forms of support for all superintendents and principals will be needed. As a result, a task force has been formed to look into new ways in which practicing administrators can receive professional development and support.

The planning committee includes several practicing administrators from around the state. Leslie Chin, a superintendent from the northern part of the state, is part of the group, along with Roosevelt Adams, a principal in her district. So is Glenn Burbank, a personnel director from Shadyville. Other principals include Roberto Garcia, Rachel Gilcrest, Tom Pistola, Frank Auschlander, and Sharee Daniels. It was a remarkable coincidence that all of these individuals were selected as part of the new committee, because all had become involved in mentoring programs in their own school districts during the past year. As a result, the work of the committee quickly focused on the potential applications and values of administrator mentoring as a form of professional development.

All the members of the committee had positive experiences with their mentoring programs. In some cases, the programs were designed to meet the specific needs of beginning principals; in others, the programs were designed to support all of the administrators in the district. For Leslie Chin, mentoring has been a way for her to learn more about the role of the superintendent by working with a colleague from a neighboring school district. Despite the general belief of all of the committee members that mentoring was effective, there was also a realization that effectiveness was being defined only in the sense that individual administrators had enjoyed their experiences. Had the programs really been successful, and were they worth the effort of continuing them in the future or starting programs in other districts across the state? These were the important issues that the statewide committee now had to address as it made a series of recommendations to the governing body of the association.

Evaluation Questions

As a school district tries to determine whether or not its mentoring program is successful, it might wish to review the following basic questions:

- **Was the program effective?** This question asks whether or not the program appeared to meet the goals and objectives that were selected in its initial development. According to this criterion, how effective has your program been in addressing the goals and objectives that were first identified by your district mentoring planning team (as described in Part I)?

_____

_____

_____

_____

_____

_____

A number of different strategies can be used to help you answer this question in your school system. For example, you might wish to design a survey questionnaire that asks those who have been involved in the mentoring program (either as mentors or protégés) to rate how effective the program was in meeting its stated objectives. Or, it might be possible to conduct interviews of program participants to determine their perceptions. This step in the evaluation process is quite obviously dependent upon the extent to which the goals and objectives that were first stated for the program were clearly stated and realistic.

- **How expensive was the program?** What costs were incurred as a result of the new mentoring program? For example, was it necessary to carry out special in-service and training sessions? Did you have to hire external consultants to help with the development of your program? How much time was spent on developing the program?

How much did the new mentoring program cost your school district to plan and implement?

_____

_____

_____

_____

_____

_____

As you respond to this question, remember to take into account the expenditures of non-monetary resources (such as time). It is nearly impossible to determine whether the cost of the program is completely worth it, but you should be able to know how much you have spent in the areas of program planning and implementation.

- **Did the program meet the needs of all of the participants?** Again, this situation is difficult to judge, particularly if you have a large number of mentors and protégés who are participating in your district's program. Nevertheless, it is important to try to determine how those who were mentored and those who served as mentors perceived their experiences.

How well do you believe that your program met the individual learning and developmental needs of the individuals who participated by serving as mentors and protégés?

_____

_____

_____

_____

_____

_____

As noted previously, you might design a questionnaire to be distributed to all principals, or you might simply wish to interview those who were involved in the program. Both techniques will give you useful information to help you decide whether all of your hard work appeared to be worth it (at least, in terms of stated criteria).

- **Did your mentoring program meet the needs of the school system?** A good mentoring program has the capability to add something to the school district in which it is developed and implemented.

To what extent do you believe your mentoring program helped the district meet its needs?

_____

_____

_____

_____

_____

_____

The best way to respond to this question is to examine the mission statement or operating philosophy of your district as a whole and decide whether or not the mentoring program has had a relationship with these statements. You might also wish to look at the goals and objectives of the school board for this year, the superintendent's goals, or the stated professional development objectives for the school system.

- **Did the program really help the protégés?** Chapter 1 listed some of the common benefits of mentoring programs as expressed by those who have been mentored. Has your program achieved some of those objectives?

  What are some of the perceived benefits achieved by protégés in your school system during the past year?

  _____

  _____

  _____

  _____

  _____

  _____

Again, the principal way in which you can get answers to this question involves talking directly with those who were the beneficiaries of the mentoring process. You might wish to interview all of the administrators who were mentored during the past year to determine whether their personal and professional goals were achieved as a result of the mentoring program.

- **Was the overall school system helped as a result of the mentoring program?** In short, did you find that your school district was more effective in achieving many of its goals and objectives because the mentoring program was in place to assist school administrators? Was it a better place for children to learn and grow because mentoring took place for the school district's leaders?

  To what extent did the adoption of a mentoring program in your school system improve the overall quality of the district?

  _____

  _____

  _____

  _____

  _____

  _____

As you respond to this question, think about not only the intended ways in which the quality of your school district was improved after you planned and implemented the program, but also consider some of the unintended ways in which life in your school district has become better (or worse) after having started the mentoring program.

- **Have you addressed program weaknesses as well as program strengths?** There is often a tendency to focus on those features of a program that have worked exceptionally well. To get a complete picture of the effectiveness of a program, you should also recognize areas that can be improved in the future.

What are some of the areas that you believe your program needs to improve on in the future?

_____

_____

_____

_____

_____

If you have identified certain weaknesses in your program, you need to take action quickly in order to ensure that these types of concerns do not destroy your efforts the next time the mentoring program is offered in your district.

- **Were participants in the program provided an opportunity to work together as a way to grow professionally?** Remember that one of the main goals of implementing a mentoring program has been to reduce the sense of isolation that is traditionally experienced by school administrators. Did you unintentionally add to this feeling by keeping your mentors apart from one another? Did you enable protégés to get together as a group?

In what ways did your program promote collegial relationships among all participants?

_____

_____

_____

_____

_____

_____

Something that might be obvious but that is often overlooked is that everyone needs support from others. In other words, do not forget that mentors also need mentors—and those who are mentored do not always need the direct intervention of their formal mentors. They can also learn and grow from others in a similar situation.

- **Did you allow ample opportunity for program participants to provide input into the overall assessment of your program?** Have you listened to those who are on the firing line? In what ways have you accounted for ongoing input from program participants as a way to improve the mentoring program in your school district?

_____

_____

_____

_____

_____

It is critical for people who are involved with any activity of professional development to have input into the design, structure, and ways in which that activity is carried out. Mentoring for school administrators is not an exception to that rule.

A few additional thoughts are offered concerning effective assessment practices to be applied to your review of the mentoring program in your district. Any effective evaluation program will provide evidence of the following:

- Collaborative efforts
- Participant involvement
- Thoughtful planning activities

- A practical and well-designed delivery system
- Attention to local implementation issues

Checking Your Plan

How well does your mentoring program and its strategy for evaluation measure up to the criteria that are identified as part of the planning process checklist noted in Chapter 2:

A. Phases of program evaluation

   1. Context evaluation

      a. Is there a plan for identifying environmental factors that might affect your mentoring program or its outcomes?

         _____ Yes   _____ No

      b. Does the plan include methods for measuring the effects of these factors on the mentoring program and its outcomes?

         _____ Yes   _____ No

      c. Are there provisions for determining whether the program needs assessment has correctly identified the needs of mentors and of all district administrators?

         _____ Yes   _____ No

   2. Input evaluation

      a. Are there provisions for evaluating your written program?

         _____ Yes   _____ No

      b. Are there provisions for evaluating the appropriateness and adequacy of human and material resources that are assigned to the mentoring program?

         _____ Yes   _____ No

   3. Process evaluation

      a. Are there provisions for determining whether the mentoring program has been implemented according to your stated program goals?

         _____ Yes   _____ No

b. If any components of the mentoring program have not been implemented according to your program plan, are there provisions for identifying the lack of implementation?

_____ Yes _____ No

c. Are there provisions for identifying the effects of the lack of implementation?

_____ Yes _____ No

4. Outcomes evaluation

a. Is there a plan to measure whether or not program objectives have been met?

_____ Yes _____ No

b. Is there a plan to measure positive and negative unintended program outcomes?

_____ Yes _____ No

5. Are there provisions for analyzing data from each phase of the program evaluation and for synthesizing the results of that analysis in a comprehensive evaluation report?

_____ Yes _____ No

B. Are there procedures for revising the mentoring program in response to the program evaluation?

_____ Yes _____ No

C. Are human resources identified in order to coordinate and implement program evaluation and revision?

_____ Yes _____ No

D. Are material resources identified that are necessary for program evaluation?

_____ Yes _____ No

Summarizing the Chapter

No matter how strongly you might wish to protect and keep any program, it is always necessary to make certain that your wishes are supported with some evidence that the program was worth it. Whatever that worth is, maybe you can identify the worth in advance before critics find their own criteria for assessment. As a result, this chapter strongly urged you to make certain that a clear and rational evaluation plan is firmly in place prior to your implementation of a mentoring program for the school administrators in your district. Failure to follow this step will likely lead to a failure of your hard work over time.

11

What Is Next?

GLENN BURBANK was really pleased with the work that had taken place in the school district during the past year. After the superintendent had directed him to develop a mentoring program as part of the new district's emphasis on administrative professional development, things had moved quite smoothly. Glenn had brought together a mentoring planning team, and that group had done a great job of planning the program. They also remained together throughout this past year to help coordinate things, to oversee the actual implementation of the program, and also to lead the evaluation process. Last week, the team presented the results of the program evaluation to the board of education. The board seemed satisfied that mentoring was effective enough to justify support for at least one more year of the program. In fact, one of the things that Glenn was responsible for doing today was to contact consultants to plan the mentor training program that would take place later this summer.

Everything looked as if the mentoring program in this district was so successful that Glenn Burbank would be quite relaxed today. But he was not. He had a strong sense that the work had only started and that he would have a very busy time this summer and all of next year.

Moving Beyond Starting a Program

There is a great tendency, whenever energy has been expended on a particular effort, to relax soon after that effort is completed. Planning for and implementing a mentoring program for the school administrators in your district represents such an activity. As stated throughout this book, program planning and development require a lot of hard work on the part of many different people. And those who are actively involved in the program as mentors and protégés must spend a considerable amount of time and energy on their work if the program is to be effective. After one year, there can be a tendency to breathe a sigh of relief and simply let the next year happen. Unfortunately, that kind of attitude will do little to ensure that all of the current year's hard work will return many benefits to your school district.

One of the most disappointing things about program development in education in general, whether it involves a new curriculum, teaching practices, or professional development programs, is that it is often viewed as a process that has a very short life span. Experienced educators are well aware of the fact that in certain school systems, change is represented by a series of gimmicks that seem to come and go every year. It is not unusual to hear educators reflect on activities in their school systems in terms of which programs lasted how long and in which years ("Last year, we did total quality management, and the year before that, we were into site-based management"). Lay public and professional educators both are faced with an endless and bewildering array of disconnected activities characterized by jargon and buzzwords. It is therefore not surprising that many innovations in education do not seem to have much of an impact on improvement, and this situation results in understandable skepticism and cynicism on the part of many people.

When adopting a mentoring program for the administrators in your school system, you should consider the program as only a small part of a total professional development program for your leadership team. There are numerous cases of school systems embracing the concept of mentoring as some sort of ornament to be added to the activities of a district without much thought to how it fits into the total scheme. In those cases, it is not surprising to find out that the mentoring program has not survived beyond a year or two. Answering the question of what to do after mentoring must be based on a serious review of the overall vision of professional development in a school system.

How Does Professional Development Fit?

An unfortunate but well-known reality is that when times are tough in school systems (for example, when funding is reduced), one of the first activities to disappear is support for staff development and in-service education. That statement is true for programs for teachers as well, and it is even truer for professional development for school administrators. Many people recognize that such a stance is shortsighted, but little is done to change things so that there is recognition of professional development for teachers and that the program is more than some sort of frill.

One of the reasons why the public might have such a negative view of the importance of professional development activities for educators is because we rarely spend time articulating in our own minds the purposes and priorities that are associated with learning programs for the adults in our schools. It is critical for any district to periodically review its vision of developmental activities for its leadership team and then base its program development on this vision. After that is in place, it might be possible to add a mentoring program or any other type of special activity that is dedicated to the improvement of leadership.

Reviewing Local Priorities

To begin the process of determining what is being done at the local district level for the professional development of school administrators, it might be helpful to think about local responses to the following questions. This process might be viewed as similar to the development of an educational platform for a school district:

1. What is your vision of effective leadership in your district?

2. What is your local district's vision of school effectiveness?

3. What are your expectations regarding the ways in which administrators would support this local vision of effectiveness?

4. What is the relationship between existing priorities for the district and new initiatives in administrative professional development for your leadership team?

5. How does your program for administrative professional development overlap or connect with ongoing professional development activities for classroom teachers?

The great concern is that a district might simply initiate mentoring for school administrators as an add-on program that has no real connection to daily life in a school system. It cannot be viewed as something that is a luxury (without any real impact on those essential features of schooling related to student learning). Not only will the public be offended by such a vision, but administrators themselves—as the clients of a mentoring program—are not likely to support activities that detract from the time that is available for their primary work.

What Happens After Mentoring?

Another recommended course of action to ensure that mentoring is not a kind of add-on activity that is unrelated to the essential activities of a school system is to work out a way to make certain that the mentoring program will persist. You can perform this task by establishing a structure to support the maintenance of mentoring in the future.

One example of such a structural support is the institutionalization of the mentor role as an ongoing position in the school system. Districts often designate a few administrators as mentors for a year, then identify others to serve in this role in the next year of a program. Mentoring in such a context becomes viewed as a rotated honor, rather than as a core responsibility to be carried out by those who have special training and expertise. Mentoring is hard work, and it should not be used only as a ceremonial award to an administrator for long service.

Another recommendation is that once you have established certain administrators in your district as professional development mentors, you need to make an effort to bring these individuals together on a regular basis in order to maintain enthusiasm (and again, to institutionalize the role of the mentor). Part of the time that is spent in the sessions can be devoted to social events that focus on the needs of administrative mentors to interact with others, and part of the time can be directed toward learning activities that will help practicing mentors fine-tune their skills.

What might be some additional ways in which your district could provide ongoing support for those who are designated as mentors?

_____

_____

_____

_____

Checking Your Plan

Review your responses to the following checklist to see how well you have planned for life after mentoring in your school district:

A. Mentors

　　1. Are provisions made for formal and informal ongoing mentor needs assessments?

　　_____ Yes _____ No

　　2. Are provisions made for modifying mentor training or mentor support as a result of the mentor needs assessment that is administered during the first year of implementation?

　　_____ Yes _____ No

B. Are human resources identified in order to coordinate and implement mentor needs assessment and corresponding modifications in the mentoring program?

_____ Yes _____ No

C. Are material resources identified that are necessary to carry out mentor needs assessment?

_____ Yes _____ No

Summarizing the Chapter

This concluding chapter was designed to help you think about what the next steps will be after you have initiated a mentoring program for school administrators in your school district. There is a great tendency, based on all of the hard work that is associated with the initial program implementation, to forget about the need to build long-lasting support for any innovative effort. It is absolutely critical that you do not waste your efforts by not deciding in these earliest stages to commit your district to a lasting vision of professional development. That is the true value of what has been presented throughout the chapters in this book.

Appendix A
Answers to the Mentoring Background Quiz in Chapter 1

1. **False.** Effective mentoring programs are designed so that both protégés and mentors benefit as a result of mutually enhancing positive interactions and support.

2. **False.** Those who have spent more time in a certain role are not necessarily more effective in that role. That is, they are not automatically better mentors. Besides, there is more to mentoring than simply showing another person how to carry out a certain task.

3. **True.** Effective mentoring should help people grow both professionally and personally.

4. **True.** Research shows that particularly in the field of school administration, women tend to place a higher value than men on all types of interpersonal relationships. This statement does not mean that men cannot or will not benefit from mentors or that all women are necessarily effective mentors, however.

5. **True.** Those who participate in a mentoring relationship one time are likely to serve in similar programs in the future. Also, those who are mentored tend to become mentors to others in the future.

6. **True.** The essence of effective mentoring is that it must involve the development of mutual trust and commitment on the part of both the mentor and the protégé.

7. **False.** Because of the complexity of most professional roles (such as the school administrator), it is likely that a person will need multiple mentors during his or her career. Such a practice will also reduce the likelihood that a person will develop too great a dependency on only one individual.

8. **False.** No interpersonal relationship, particularly one that is as intensive as an effective mentor-protégé relationship, will be so perfect and smooth as to involve no conflict at all.

9. **False.** There are many ways of matching mentors and protégés. Making use of similar job titles and job descriptions is one approach but is certainly not the only effective strategy that can be used.

10. **True.** Many different benefits can be derived from an effective mentoring relationship.

11. **True.** Mentoring can involve a number of different professional development activities that are negotiated between a mentor and a protégé. Mentoring is not solely a one-to-one conversation between a mentor and a protégé.

12. **True.** There are many different and important relationships available to school leaders, such as career guides, peer pals, and so forth.

13. **False.** Mentoring is based on effective performance of a job.

14. **True.** Because mentors and protégés often form extremely powerful bonds, it is easy for expectations to be high. Nevertheless, it is critical for both partners to remain realistic about the nature of their relationships.

15. **False.** The most effective mentors are those individuals who engage in a process of discovery with their protégés. Effective mentors are able to ask the right questions but are not always able to provide all of the right answers.

Appendix B

Mentoring Scenarios

THE FOLLOWING SCENARIOS have been provided to enable you to practice some of the mentoring skills described throughout this book. Describe the kinds of things that you and your protégé would talk about in a session. What strategies might be used next in your meeting?

1. You are an elementary school principal who has several years of experience in your school system. The superintendent has recently asked you to serve as a mentor in a new program that is designed to prepare teachers in your district for future administrative roles. One of the interns is a fourth-grade teacher in your building. You are pleased to assume this role for at least two reasons. First, the request came directly from the superintendent. Second, you realize that only one other principal in the district has been asked to serve, so this opportunity is an honor for you. You have asked your fourth-grade teacher to stop in after school today to talk about this new program. You know little about its structure or what you are actually supposed to do now that you are a mentor.

2. This first-year principal was a teacher in the district for 10 years before going into administration. In fact, the principal taught in the same building. The concern that the principal expresses to you is that there appears to be no one to talk to in the building. No one is friendly in the same way that people were the year before.

3. This central office administrator was considered an effective middle school principal in your district for a number of years before he moved into his present position. He has had no previous special training in the area of central office administration. The primary reason why this person was placed in his present position was because, as a close friend of the new superintendent, he was viewed as a close confidant who could be trusted when many of the other central office administrators were still too close to the former superintendent. The problem

that the administrator shares with you is that he really felt competent as a principal but not in his new role. Your protégé is extroverted and is concerned primarily with organizational goals and task accomplishment.

4. This individual has been a principal in your district for nearly 20 years. She has been recognized as a leader among the district administrators, and the community often looks to her as an unofficial spokesperson—frequently ignoring pronouncements from the central office. This person has long been recognized for strong skills as a disciplinarian who knows how to keep the teachers in line and who has served as an effective building manager. A major shift in district priorities started a year earlier with the election of several new school board members who, in turn, replaced the former superintendent with a new administrator who has a Ph.D. This superintendent was deliberately hired because the board wanted someone to reorder the priorities of the district. They wanted a strong instructional leader who would, in turn, make changes in the leadership patterns of the other administrators in the district. Now, this experienced principal is concerned that she is on the superintendent's hit list and that she will not fit in with the district's new priorities. A transfer to another district is not likely, and early retirement is not possible.

5. This principal has moved to your rural district after six years as an assistant principal in a school that is in a rather affluent suburban school district. She expresses a good deal of frustration on a continuing basis over a lack of financial support from the community and also over the lower expectations that parents seem to have regarding the role of schools in preparing students for future academic pursuits.

6. This experienced principal has recently moved into your district. She is the only female administrator in your district, and she confides in you that she feels very uncomfortable working with the "good old boys," most of whom have worked together for many years. Several were coaches together, and they still meet on Friday afternoons at the Locker Room Bar and Grill to socialize and to talk business about schools.

7. This first-year principal simply cannot find enough time to do all of the things that are being expected of administrators in the district. You know that he is extremely intelligent, and everybody who encounters this person finds him to be pleasant, eager, and enthusiastic—apparently a real winner. But the principal has told you that he is very frustrated because all of his personal priorities have taken a backseat to the job. In fact, he has indicated that he is thinking about going back to the classroom next year.

8. This principal has recently experienced a number of personal crises. His spouse left him after more than 20 years of marriage. People have noted that as a

response, he has become extremely moody and has withdrawn from social contact with the teaching staff, with other administrators, and with members of the community. This situation is a complete reversal of the pattern that was demonstrated by this principal for many years. He was always the life of the party at meetings. The rumor mill suggests that this principal has also started to drink to excess.

9. This principal, who has seven years of experience at the elementary school level, has recently become the center of community controversy. A fourth-grade student in the school has been identified as HIV-positive, but the name of the student has been kept secret. There is a great demand on the principal by parents and others who want him to reveal the name of the student "in order to protect the other kids and teachers who must work with the poor child."

10. This superintendent is generally recognized as one of the truly bright young superintendents in the state. She is nearing the completion of a Ph.D. at a local university, and the school board believes that she is a very good leader. The reputation that is heard from the superintendent's subordinates, however, is that she has many good ideas and a great vision for where the district might go, but she rarely follows through with an implementation plan. In short, the expression "all talk, no action" is beginning to be heard about her in the district.

Appendix C

Mentor-Protégé Action Planning Form

Protégé name: _____

Mentor name: _____

Three major goals for this year:

1. _____

2. _____

3. _____

Objectives	*Learning Activities*	*Outcome Measures*

Suggested Readings

THE FOLLOWING MATERIALS might be helpful for you as you begin to learn more about the concept of mentoring and how it can be applied to professional development programs for school leaders:

Alvy, Harvey and Robbins, Pam, (1998). *If I only knew: Success strategies for navigating the principalship.* Thousand Oaks, CA: Corwin.

Barnett, Bruce G., (1985). Peer-assisted leadership: A stimulus for professional growth. *Thrust*, 14, pp. 48–49.

Bova, Breda M. and Phillips, R. R., (1984). Mentoring as a learning experience for adults. *Journal of Teacher Education*, 35 (3), pp. 196–210.

Crow, Gary M. and Matthews, L. Joseph, (1998). *Finding one's way: How mentoring can lead to dynamic leadership.* Thousand Oaks, CA: Corwin.

Daloz, Laurent A., (1999). *Mentor.* (2nd ed.) San Francisco: Jossey-Bass.

Daresh, John C. (in press). *Beginning the principalship: A practical guide for new school leaders.* (2nd ed.) Thousand Oaks, CA: Corwin.

Gardiner, Mary E., Enomoto, Ernestine, and Groza, Margaret, (2000). *Coloring outside the lines: Mentoring women into school leadership.* Albany: State University of New York Press.

Jerome, Paul, (1994). *Coaching through effective feedback.* Irvine, CA: Richard Chang Associates.

Keirsey, David and Bates, Marilyn. (1984). *Please understand me: Character and temperament types.* Del Mar, CA: Gnosology.

Kerka, S., (1998). New Perspectives on Mentoring. (ERIC Digest No. 194). Columbus, OH: ERIC Clearinghouse on Adult, Career, and Vocational Education.

Kolb, David A., (1984). *Experiential learning: Experience as the source of learning and development.* Englewood Cliffs, NJ: Prentice Hall.

Kram, Kathy, (1988). *Mentoring at work: Developmental relationships in organizational life.* Lanham, MD: University Press of America.

Lawrence, Gordon, (1982). *People types and tiger stripes: A practical guide to learning styles.* Gainesville, FL: Center for Applications of Psychological Types.

Murray, Margo and Owen, Marna, (1991). *Beyond the myths and magic of mentoring.* San Francisco: Jossey-Bass.

Myers, Isabel, (1962). *Manual: The Myers-Briggs type indicator.* Palo Alto, CA: Consulting Psychologists Press.

Reiman, Alan J. and Theis-Sprinthall, Lois, (1998). *Mentoring and supervision for teacher development.* New York: Longman.

Zey, Michael G., (1991). *The mentor connection.* New Brunswick, NJ: Transaction Publishers.

Index

CORWIN
PRESS

The Corwin Press logo—a raven striding across an open book—represents the happy union of courage and learning. We are a professional-level publisher of books and journals for K–12 educators, and we are committed to creating and providing resources that embody these qualities. Corwin's motto is "Success for All Learners."